ST GEORGE

ST GEORGE
A SAINT FOR ALL

✠

SAMANTHA RICHES

REAKTION BOOKS

For my parents – John William Riches and Olivia Erskine Riches

Published by Reaktion Books Ltd
33 Great Sutton Street
London EC1V ODX, UK
www.reaktionbooks.co.uk

First published 2015
Copyright © Samantha Riches 2015

Printed and bound in Great Britain
by TJ International, Padstow, Cornwall

A catalogue record for this book is available from the British Library

ISBN 978 1 78023 451 9

Contents

Ethiopian priest with images of St George
and other saints, late 20th century.

Introduction: 'God is Great but Not Like St George'

This rather startling expression was attributed to the Kouranis, who are Lebanese Christians, as recently as 2008.[1] For all its apparent challenge to the Supreme Being, my initial reaction to it was less concerned with what could seem to some readers to be inherent blasphemy than with the way it resonated with my own experience.

Intensive study into the cult of this hugely important, wildly popular and frequently misunderstood figure can lead to the conclusion that St George has been constructed to operate on many levels: as an heroic human battling a monstrous foe; as a suffering martyr who transcends many of the conventional limits of human bodies and earthly existence; and as a mythic character who challenges overly neat understandings of the distances between religious traditions both within and beyond Christianity. The extent to which this has been a deliberate, considered process of construction is debatable – the simple fact that his cult is so widespread and has been deeply ingrained within belief systems for more than 1,700 years tends to suggest that there has been no grand plan for encouraging his devotion. If anything the evidence points the other way, with attempts to challenge and suppress his cult appearing from as early as the fifth century CE. St George has been frequently reinvented in ways that can surprise and sometimes even offend, but he has never slipped into obscurity.

The fact that St George was acclaimed as a saint well before the concept of formal canonization was invented is both his strength and his weakness. He is always susceptible to the charge that he is not a 'proper' saint – who on earth could believe in even half the stories associated with him? Yet it may well be that the impossibility of pinning him down to one simple narrative is actually the seat of his power to attract a following of such fervour, for the flexibility of the figure allows him to respond to a wide range of needs and motivations.

By far the most well-known legend associated with St George is the story of how he encountered and slew a fierce dragon in order to rescue a princess. He is by no means the only Christian dragon-slayer: his best-known comrade in this activity is St Michael, but there are many others, including popular figures of the early Church such as St Martha (whose intervention led to the death of the Tarasque, according to a Provençal legend), as well as more obscure saints such as the Cornish St Carantoc (who triumphed over a monster which had outwitted even the great King Arthur). Despite the motif's prevalence, it is important to note that St George's dragon-slaying adventure is by no means all there is to his story – in fact there is no mention of the monster in versions of his legend from the first millennium, other than in metaphoric description of a heathen emperor who put him on trial for refusing to give up his Christian beliefs.

Where the dragon-slaying story does appear as part of the narrative there is little consistency in the chronology of events. In fact, the dragon narrative often appears as a kind of bolt-on floating element, which can be presented as part of the saint's legend if required. An example of this approach is found in the following version of the life of the saint:

> The man who was to become known as St George was born around 280 CE to a wealthy Christian family of noble origin, in the 'city of Capadocia [*sic*]' in Asia Minor. He followed the usual career of a young nobleman and joined the Roman army, where his ability and charm brought him quick promotion to the rank of tribune in the Imperial Guard. According to some stories he was a friend of Constantine, later to become the first Christian Roman emperor, and travelled with him to Britain to visit holy places such as Glastonbury and Caerleon. He returned to Nicomedia, the capital of the Eastern Roman Empire before Byzantium took this honour.

There he met the fierce persecution of the reign of Diocletian (r. 284–305 CE).

A formal edict against Christianity was promulgated on 23 February 303, and a notice to this effect was published the following day. All churches were to be levelled to the ground, all sacred books would be burned, all Christians who held any honourable rank were to be degraded and deprived of civil rights, and all Christians who were not already officials would be reduced to slavery.

With great courage, a young man pushed his way through the market to read the proclamation, and then in front of the awestruck crowd he deliberately tore down the imperial edict and threw it away. This man has been popularly identified as St George. In spite of this act of defiance the edict was proclaimed and the great church in Nicomedia was ransacked and destroyed by the Praetorian Guard. St George liberated his slaves, distributed all his wealth to the poor and prepared himself for martyrdom. He entered Diocletian's palace and rebuked him for his behaviour against the Christians. Diocletian tried to seduce the young man away from his Christian beliefs with promises that he would be granted a higher position in the empire. When these promises failed, George was threatened with unbearable tortures and imprisoned. Diocletian arranged for a beautiful woman to try to debauch him in his prison cell; St George not only resisted her charms but also converted her to Christianity.

The following morning the failure of the plot was discovered and the woman was executed. Diocletian then ordered that St George should be subjected to a whole series of physical torments. This Coptic version states that there were many tortures, including tearing his flesh with metal spikes and being buried in quicklime. Some of these sufferings culminated in the saint's death; his subsequent resurrection by Christ led to the conversion of many pagans. Diocletian decided that St George was using magic, so he called his best magician, and told him to prepare a lethal poison. The young man made the sign of the cross before drinking from the offered cup, so no harm came to him. He was given a second cup of the poison while his hands were bound behind his back, but the young man contrived to make the sign of the cross again by pointing with his head and asking: 'Shall I drink it from here, or here, or here, or here?'

Throughout all these tortures, and despite all his suffering, St George kept on talking to Diocletian about the powers of the Christian faith. Finally the emperor asked him if he could raise someone from the dead. The saint intoned a prayer over a dead man, who came back to life. This led to the conversion of the resurrected man and the magician, as well as many others: all were executed. Diocletian then offered to make the young man a prince, if he would sacrifice once to the idols. He replied: 'Tomorrow you will see the powers of your gods.'

The following day crowds of people went to the temple to witness St George's sacrifice to the idols, and many were converted when he caused the idols to fall. At this the emperor and his men put an end to the lives of the new Christians, the converted Empress Alexandra and the young man himself on 23 Baramouda [April] 303. The saint's body was buried in his mother's home, which was on the seashore at Lydda, in Palestine. Before long, though, his fame had spread all over the world. Constantine, who succeeded Diocletian as emperor, stated that St George was the true model of the young Christian, and ordered a church to be built over his grave. In Egypt the Copts called him 'The Prince of Martyrs' and built more than 200 churches named in his honour. He is thought of as a personal friend by the majority of the Copts, who believe in the power of his prayers for them.

The legend of the dragonslaying is the most famous story associated with St George, and it occurred when St George was stationed with the Roman army in Libya. In that area a dragon – which was described as a huge crocodile with scaled wings – had eaten so many of the people that everyone fled the countryside for the city of Salone to take shelter behind its walls.

The dragon's breath was so poisonous that as it snored over the city wall people would drop dead. To keep the beast away, each day two sheep were tethered some distance from the wall. Eventually the supply of sheep ran low and the miserable people could think of no alternative but to sacrifice one child every day instead, chosen by drawing lots. One day the lot fell on the king's daughter, Sabra, a girl of fourteen. Dressed in her most splendid clothes, as if for her wedding, the unfortunate girl was taken outside the city walls. While she was awaiting her fate, weeping, St George the tribune came along, mounted on his white horse. On hearing her tragic story he decided to kill the dragon. 'Fair girl,' he said, 'do not be afraid for I will save your life with the aid of my lord Jesus Christ.' When the dragon appeared St George engaged it in combat, wounding it with his lance so badly that it could fight no longer. Then he and Sabra tied a rope around its neck and dragged it to the town. In the marketplace, George beheaded it in front of the cheering inhabitants, and the people were all baptized as Christians.

This version is drawn from the beliefs of the Coptic church,[2] a religious tradition now primarily associated with Nubia (which can be approximated to modern-day Egypt) and Ethiopia; this legend reflects the very strong devotion which the saint attracts to this day in Ethiopia (see p. 6 for a twentieth-century ritual object featuring St George among a group of other Christian saints and deities). There is no evidence that any of this actually took place, but the act of attempting to resist the persecution of Christians under Diocletian does seem to be the kernel of the Christian tradition of St George.

We have here a contemporary version of the narrative which presents a story that is at once both strange and familiar. Many readers will already have at least a passing acquaintance with the dragon story but far fewer will be aware of the martyrdom legend, let alone the narrative of the tearing down of the edict banning Christianity. St George's status as a liberator of prisoners is recognized in many places where his cult is strong, yet few of his devotees will identify him as someone who freed his own slaves.

Even the version of the dragon legend presented here is by no means standard – the princess is not typically named (and in Ethiopia she is usually called Biruwit, not Sabra), the location is usually identified as Silene (a place no more historically authentic than 'Salone'), and the dragon is generally described as meek and subdued as it is led, rather than dragged against its will, into the city. The concept of a dragon breathing pestilence is quite common, but the image of one snoring over the city walls is probably unique. The anonymous author of the narrative from which this version is drawn comments, apparently without irony, that this story seems to be exaggerated, suggesting that St George may actually have fought an ordinary crocodile. This detail may reflect the North African context, both of the dragon story and the Coptic Christian tradition more generally. In the same way the story presented here of his birth and life as a soldier are by no means standard – there are many names in circulation for his parents, and a number of locations claimed for his birth, ranging from Lydda/Lod in the Holy Land to Tintagel in Cornwall;[3] the assertion that St George was a friend of Constantine and visited Glastonbury seems to have arisen in the nineteenth century as part of an effort to identify links between England and its patron saint.

On one level the story of St George and the dragon represents the Christianization of a fundamental human myth – the archetype of the hero who fights a monster and prevails, usually to rescue a maiden, is found throughout recorded human cultures. In ancient Egypt an obvious parallel is found in the motif of Horus and the crocodile. This hawk-headed god is often depicted hunting another god named Set, or Setekh, who appeared in the form of a crocodile or serpent. Set was Horus's uncle (he is occasionally said to be Horus's brother), and he had murdered Horus's father Osiris, so the legend works as a revenge tragedy as well as the triumph of good over evil. It is sometimes claimed that St George's dragon-slaying exploits are derived directly from this myth, and this assertion is given weight by some images with a Graeco-Roman influence where Horus is shown on horseback, in contravention of the usual Egyptian approach, which does not include depictions of deities on horses.[4] Given the Eastern Mediterranean location which seems to be the origin of St George's cult, it is entirely credible that an Egyptian myth would have had a role to play in shaping this Christianized figure. However, as the Coptic account makes clear, St George was much more than a dragon-slayer – he was a martyr, a healer, a liberator and a figure of youth and chastity.

St George is annually criticized, even vilified; as his feast day, 23 April, draws near, what feels like an inevitable process of public scrutiny takes place, invariably involving the wearying rehearsal of mistaken beliefs. St George is perhaps unique in the extent to which he is universally recognized and yet also a profoundly misunderstood and misappropriated figure. I am periodically called upon to defend St George in the media – for example, when proponents of St Edward the Confessor, St Edmund, St Alban, St Augustine of Canterbury, St Cuthbert or other 'more appropriate' saints are given space to put forward the contention that their own preferred candidate should be named as the English patron saint while St George is sidelined as a relic of empire – and am always surprised by the extent to which people seem to think that they understand him and what he represents, and how easily they are tempted to cast him aside.[5] His detractors often 'know' that he was Turkish, even though Turkey as a country did not exist in the early fourth century when he is generally said to have lived, and the earliest evidence for his cult relates to Syria. Equally, they fixate on his associations with the imperialism of the late nineteenth and early twentieth centuries (an important but actually quite small element in the history of his cult), and are often unaware of the fact that devotion to St George reached Britain as early as the seventh century, or that he was not described as a dragon-slayer for the first 700 years of his cult, and that in the oldest surviving version of the saint's life in English (by Ælfric, in the late tenth century) he is not even a soldier.

The intention of this book is to defamiliarize St George, to challenge the sense that what he represents is obvious to all. It is only by dissecting and questioning the concepts that we *think* we know that we can come truly to understand their diversity and complexity. We need to attempt a holistic understanding of St George if we are to appreciate the potential he has to act as a positive and inclusive symbol with a role to play in the important arena of national identity. St George has been identified at the patron saint of many countries and locales as various as Ethiopia, Georgia, Catalonia, Syria, many towns in Italy and France, and the Roma people, to name but a few. Many English people who express concern about the role of St George as a national symbol are totally unaware of this extensive web of patronages and connections; they also tend to have very little knowledge of the overwhelmingly positive connotations that this saint has in the wider world, both within and beyond a whole range of Christian traditions.

This book aims to help the reader to disentangle St George from some of the concepts that have become associated with him over the last 1,700 years, and to appreciate them as aspects of a changeable, malleable, dynamic cult whose elements and emphases have ebbed and flowed over time. One of the most significant canards challenged is that St George should be seen as a fixed and immutable symbol of a lost 'England' of white Anglo-Saxon heritage, a figure whom it would be heretical to present as a black man, a gay man, a woman, a non-Christian – the truth is that St George has been represented in all these guises, and many others, even back as far as the eighth century. England is now, and has been for many centuries, a diverse country with an array of cultures, ethnicities, sexualities, genders and belief systems. St George is able to encompass all these multiplicities, and we are all demeaned by any attempt – well-meaning or otherwise – to cast him as no more than a fabricated vision of a golden-haired, blue-eyed 'English of the English'.[6] It is clear that St George has a devotion that is largely independent of English claims to his patronage and this book explores some of the major themes which manifest themselves in the cult of St George across different times and cultures: we will find him as a healer, a miracle-worker, a guardian of seafarers, a champion of youth, a leader of armies and a breaker of sieges, as well as in the more familiar guise of dragon-slayer and princess liberator. These tropes, and many others, are explored in the following pages, and even when we think we clearly recognize him, there are often subtle variations to challenge our certainties.

I

St George: A Reappraisal for a Multicultural Age

S t George is no stranger to controversy. In the late fifth century his legend was included in the first ever index of forbidden books on the grounds that the complex martyrdom story associated with him, with its grisly tortures and multiple resurrections, is too incredible to be given credence; if this was an attempt to suppress the cult it was profoundly unsuccessful, since he is recognized around the world, and in a variety of religious traditions, as a vital component of personal and communal belief systems.

For many readers the immediate association which St George brings to mind is his status as the patron saint of England, but it is worth noting that this designation was not officially recognized until the mid-eighteenth century. Although it is entirely possible to find St George spoken of as an English patron far earlier than this, it is unlikely that he was widely recognized as a national patron of England in any meaningful way until after the Reformation; there may well have been a conscious effort to try to cement him into English affections, but the process was far from straightforward.

One of the most long-standing challenges to St George can be traced back to Edward Gibbon, author of the hugely influential work *The History of the Decline and Fall of the Roman Empire* (six volumes, 1776–89). Gibbon propagated the idea that St George could be identified with George of Cappadocia, a well-documented historical figure who pursued a career selling questionable pork to the Roman army, later rising to the position of archbishop of Alexandria. A known adherent of the Arian heresy, a belief system that questioned the divinity of Jesus, he was murdered by an angry mob in 362 CE.

Gibbon's contention was refuted with some force in an essay by Dr Samuel Pegge, presented to the Society of Antiquaries of London in 1777 and published ten years later in their journal *Archaeologia*. Despite this, and the periodic restating of the difference between St George and his heretical namesake by a range of authors, the identification of St George with George of Cappadocia still has currency today, and it is regularly put forward by people who wish to discredit St George's claims to be the national patron of England. The longevity of the misidentification can be attributed not only to the pervasive influence of Gibbon, but also to the fact that no less a figure than Ralph Waldo Emerson restated the erroneous thesis in *English Traits* (1856), despite the fact that even cursory research would have told him that Gibbon's conclusions had already been called into serious question.

If St George was not a purveyor of dodgy meat and dodgy ideas, who was he? Much intellectual effort has been expended on the question of the historical authenticity of the figure who has come to be identified as St George.[1] Suffice it to say that, whether or not anyone lived who did any of the things associated with St George – witnessing for his faith, being tortured and executed for his refusal to recant, healing the sick, repeatedly rising from the dead, freeing prisoners, protecting the young, appearing as a ghostly figure to lead armies and break sieges (and, from about the eleventh century, killing a dragon to rescue a princess) – it is clear that over many centuries a wide range of people have been taken with the idea that someone *might* have done these things. They called that someone St George, and created a lively cult around him that spread to most parts of the world from its probable origins in the early fourth century in the eastern Mediterranean.

Analogues of St George beyond Christianity

Turning away from the question of whether there is any historical reality underpinning the concept of St George, and looking at what – to me at least – is the much more fascinating question of what people have believed about him and why, we quickly come up against a concept which for many Christians, and indeed Anglophone people of all faiths and none, is both a challenge and, one hopes, a liberation. Despite the fact that St George is clearly a Christian figure, one of the most interesting facets of his cult is the way that aspects of his legend and imagery are paralleled in other, non-Christian traditions, both religious and secular.

Al-Khidr

St George has particularly strong links with an archetypal figure who appears in a number of religious traditions under a variety of names, which include Al-Khidr, Khwaja Khizr, Hizir, Pir Badar, Raja Kidar, Mar Jiryis and Jiryis Baqiya. This figure is particularly associated with the eastern Mediterranean. Thus, for example, St George is venerated by Palestinian Christians as Mar Jiryis, and the same figure is recognized by Palestinian Muslims as Al-Khidr. Furthermore, this figure is associated with, and even identified as, the prophet Elijah in some folkloric traditions within both Judaism and Islam.

There are a number of common themes which arise with this figure across religious traditions, particularly an association with immortality, healing, fertility, wisdom and water – especially the discovery of a well or fountain of eternal youth – and also the patronage and protection of people travelling by sea. The figure of Al-Khidr is also associated with rainfall, notably appearing in visions to prophesy the end of drought. One significant difference between this archetypal figure and St George is that there is usually no dragon legend attached to it – although Muslims in Palestine are known to recognize the iconography of the mounted dragon-slayer as Al-Khidr. It is likely, then, that Al-Khidr and the other analogues are more closely associated with the early understandings of St George as a holy man and martyr rather than with the later understandings of him as a dragon-slayer.

All the versions of the archetype can be referred back to figures in the folklore of ancient Sumeria and Babylon. For example, the figure of Ea, known also as Enki, was the ruler of the streams that rose in the underworld, and flowed from there to fertilize the land. In imagery Ea is linked with fish, and often holds in his hands a flowing vase which is the source of the water of immortal life. He is also identified as a figure of great wisdom. The various names applied to the holy archetype known as Al-Khidr, Mar Jiryis and so forth often equate to terms such as 'the Living', 'the Green One' and 'the Evergreen One'; he is sometimes said to derive from the Greek sea god Glaucos, whose name means 'the Blue One' or 'the Green One'. Glaucos was a fisherman who achieved immortality, and hence the status of a god, after eating a seashore herb which he had noticed restored his fish to life. Utnapishtim, a character in the Babylonian *Epic of Gilgamesh* (eighteenth century BCE), attained immortality in a remarkably similar way, and this parallel may indicate another influence.

Al-Khidr is a significant figure in some Islamic traditions, especially Sufism, but it is true to say that he is primarily a folkloric figure who is recognized to be pre-Islamic in origin. He is reputed to have found the Fountain of Youth, or the Well of Life, which is said to be located near the confluence of the Mediterranean and the Red Sea. Drinking from this well or fountain confers immortality; it is claimed that Al-Khidr was repeatedly killed and resurrected, with one story involving martyrdom at the behest of a pagan king. This seems to be evidence of a strong link to early versions of the legend of St George as a Christian martyr, which claim that he was killed and resurrected on more than one occasion, and it perhaps indicates a common source for these legends. Some traditions state that Al-Khidr bathed three times in the Well of Life: in consequence his skin and all his clothing turned entirely green, and he leaves green footprints wherever he goes. In fact, the name 'Al-Khidr' ('the Green One') can be understood as an invocation of the natural world as well as a reflection of his physicality – it is certainly a theme in the 'pagan' equivalent of St George. The immortality of Al-Khidr is sometimes interpreted as a symbol of the immensity of his knowledge and providential wisdom; we should note that the Jewish prophet Elijah is also thought to be immortal and deeply wise.

Like St George, the figure of Al-Khidr is invoked as a healer: one of his shrines, visited by adherents of Christianity and Judaism as well as Islam, is known to have been located at a kind of psychiatric asylum near Bethlehem, where several miraculous healings were claimed. Another healing shrine was located on the slopes of Mount Carmel – a site strongly associated with Elijah – while in the early twentieth century it was noted that those suffering from 'fever, quaking and fear' resorted to a Christian shrine of Mar Jiryis at Urmi in Persia. Al-Khidr's interventions in human affairs are largely meant to help and provide succour to people in times of need: indeed, the ambulance service in Turkey today is called the 'Khidr-Service'.

Al-Khidr also has strong associations with fertility, particularly in the form of stories linking him with the weather. One example dates to 1906, when the winter rains failed in Palestine, leading to famine and poverty. It is claimed that a woman was slowly filling a pitcher from a scanty spring at a place known as Ain Kârim when she was accosted by a horseman holding a long lance who ordered her to water his horse. She objected to his command, but obeyed him, and was horrified to discover that blood, and not water, streamed from the pitcher. The horseman then revealed his identity as Al-Khidr, and ordered the woman to tell everyone that if Allah had not sent the drought there would have been a great pestilence and other grave misfortunes. He then appeared to another woman at Hebron with a similar message, promising that the rains would come after the Greek New Year. It seems that his prophecy came true. This water-themed story also exemplifies the way in which Al-Khidr is recognized as an eternal wanderer who helps people in trouble.

In parts of Turkey, Iraq, Iran, Central Asia and Afghanistan people have held a special Khidr meal at home to gain his blessings. In parts of the Balkans and Turkey, Muslims have also been known to celebrate a Khidr feast, and his sanctuaries and pilgrimage sites can be found throughout the Muslim world. Seeing a vision of and meeting Al-Khidr has been regarded as a great distinction in some branches of Islam: an encounter with him has been one of the distinguishing marks of Sufi saints, just as a vision of Elijah is much sought after in some forms of Judaism. Al-Khidr is sometimes represented as an angel, reflecting both his immortality and his role as a kind of heavenly messenger; he is even described as the 'Green Angel Guide' in some Islamic writings.

Khwaja Khizr/Khadir

The figure known as Al-Khidr is understood as a kind of patron saint of travellers, also of sailors, especially in the Middle East and Northern India. In the latter area he is identified with the prophet, saint or deity known as Khwaja Khizr, Khadir (especially in parts of India which have a strong Muslim influence), Pir Badar or Raja Kidar; this figure is the object of a popular cult to this day, common to both Muslims and Hindus. There is a story that links the Indian Khadir to a healing well and – intriguingly – the 'quelling of a serpent', which may possibly indicate some link to the identification of St George as a dragon-slayer.

Elijah

The prophet Elijah, who was active in Israel in the ninth century BCE, is a favourite hero in written and oral Jewish folk literature; he is considered to be a special guardian of Israel.

Within rabbinic literature he is identified as the herald of the future redemption – he will announce the arrival of the Jewish Messiah, for example – but this motif is much less significant in folklore than an understanding of him as a heavenly figure that has been sent to Earth to combat social injustice. In many stories he rewards the poor who are hospitable to strangers and punishes the greedy rich, regardless of their status. The link between Elijah and St George may not be immediately obvious – Elijah is never presented as a knightly dragon-slayer, for example – but when some of the other aspects of the saint, such as his roles as a healer and a symbol of fertility, are borne in mind the connection becomes clearer. Meanwhile, beliefs about Elijah's powers as a healer and wise man are deeply entwined with similar understandings of Al-Khidr; in the Old Testament book of 1 Kings, and in later Talmudic literature, Elijah is described as a rainmaker, another function he shares with his Islamic counterpart. Hundreds of shrines to Elijah in the Middle East and in Greece testify to a continuing understanding of his effectiveness as a patronal figure.

Many of the stories told about Elijah can be understood as a form of social protest, while at the same time offering comfort to the poor. Elijah alleviates the burdens of Jewish communities suffering from religious and national persecution. He appears especially on the eve of Passover when he punishes misers and provides poor people with the necessaries to prepare the Seder – the ceremony observed in Jewish homes on the first night of Passover (or the second night, in the Jewish diaspora). Every household celebrating the Seder will traditionally set a place for Elijah, in expectation of his appearance, and the best cup is reserved for him. The cup of Elijah is placed in the centre of the festive table; it is usually a large ornate goblet that is filled with wine but not drunk, as an expression of a fervent hope that the prophet will come soon.

Elijah's interventions and miracles include healing, fertility and the interpretation of mysterious events and visions. Elijah's cave or shrine on Mount Carmel is claimed as the site of many healing legends. Another prevalent motif is his ability to act as provider, based on his role as a rainmaker. He conferred an inexhaustible barrel of oil on one devotee and distributed magic money-making boxes to the poor, but then took them away when the recipients stopped being charitable.

It is claimed that Elijah did not die but was raised up to heaven in a fiery chariot. He is said to have dropped his cloak as he was carried, and supernatural powers are ascribed to this garment. In some understandings he is thought to wander the earth – just as Al-Khidr does – usually disguised as a poor man. Some Jewish folk beliefs describe ways to bring about visions of Elijah, and even to meet him. His name is inscribed on many protective amulets, especially in areas influenced by Islamic culture.

Ogum

Another syncretic form of St George is recognized in the Afro-Brazilian religion Candomblé. Here we have two quite distinct traditions colliding and cross-fertilizing: Roman Catholicism and Yoruba, a belief system that originated in West African countries such as Nigeria, Benin and Togo.

Interest in St George was imported to Brazil by Portuguese colonists: devotion to the saint in Portugal can be traced back to the twelfth century, and during the reign of King John I (r. 1385–1433) he was recognized as the country's patron. Candomblé, meanwhile, is based on religious practices brought to Brazil by enslaved West Africans, and Ogum is one of the most significant deity figures in this belief system. In Yoruba mythology, Ogum is a primordial Orisha (a spirit or deity reflecting a manifestation of an aspect of the god Olodumare) whose first appearance was as a hunter. Ogum is identified as the first of the Orisha to descend to earth to find somewhere suitable for future humans to live. He is understood as an aggressively masculine and martial spirit, with a fiery temperament and an ability to heal diseases of the blood. Within Candomblé, Ogum may also be identified with St Sebastian, the soldier saint who is frequently represented shot with arrows; in the European tradition he is associated with protection from plague (since plague sores look rather like arrow wounds) and is also a locus for homoerotic projection.

St Sebastian is the official patron of Rio de Janeiro, but he is rivalled by St George in terms of public displays of interest, and the parallel of both figures with Ogum tends to reinforce the identification of these saints as locally significant. There are many songs about St George and churches are well attended on his feast day, which is identified as a time when the spiritual fight is particularly acute.

In late 2012 St George was invoked in the title of a new soap opera. *Salve Jorge* ('Hail George') is a story set partially in one of Rio de Janeiro's *favelas* – hillside shanty towns – and it sets out to reflect social problems such as human trafficking alongside the more standard melodramatic fare of love and betrayal. It is notable that the series has drawn protests from some evangelical Christian groups. It seems that their objections are twofold – they dislike the title's evocation of St George, because they feel it contradicts the biblical commandment to worship only God; they also allege that the invocation of St George is a reference to a deity in Candomblé (presumably they mean Ogum, though this is somewhat unclear) and are unhappy with this non-Christian context.

There are evangelical websites that show banners saying *Queima o Jorge* ('Burn George'), using fiery letters, and slogans such as 'Those who believe in the Lord Jesus as the only saviour will not watch this soap opera.' Meanwhile, a spokesman for the production company has said that the title is a reference to one of the characters, who is interested in St George as a warrior who stood for chivalry, and noted that the figure 'exists in all cultures, religious or not'.[2] My own feeling is that the decision to use this title for the series, and the strength of feeling in the opponents of this soap opera and its invocation of the saint, are good indicators of the extent to which St George is a significant figure in Brazilian society, both as a Christian and non-Christian archetype; there is also a clear indication of the variance in understandings which is found in a few other places with an ambivalent attitude to the saint, although I am unaware of St George attracting quite this level of active hostility outside this specific context.

The Green Man

Returning to Europe, our final example of a non-Christian analogue of the saint is found, paradoxically, physically within many medieval churches, and indeed some later ones. The haunting image of a foliate face known as the Green Man appears in carved stone corbels and woodwork such as misericords and church bench ends. These features often date from the fourteenth and fifteenth centuries, but they can be modern. Misericords in particular are identified as a liminal location; they often feature humorous, even scatological, imagery, and invocations of a secular life, such as wild people living in the woods beyond the reach of organized religion, are commonplace. It is worth noting that the Green Man motif is sometimes known as the 'Green

George': this tends to reflect an essentially extra-Christian belief system where nature is celebrated and reverenced, but also identified as threatening and needing to be placated.

There is a great deal of evidence that springtime rituals form an important part of St George's cult in many parts of Europe. The rituals are often claimed to be Christian, but it seems likely that they are a continuation, and Christianization, of an ancient ritual drawn from what can loosely be termed 'pagan' tradition. The 'Green George' festival, which is mainly celebrated in Greece and other Balkan states, is an especially clear example of an analogue of St George in a non-Christian religious tradition. In these rites of springtime the vegetation god 'Green George' is often represented by a young man clad from head to toe in green leaves; sometimes a particular tree is selected to stand as the 'Green George' and decorated with flowers. A sequence of ritual gestures that symbolize planting, harvesting and fertility is carried out, and frequently culminates with the 'Green George' figure being thrown into water. The 'Green George' festival and the feast of St George are celebrated on the same day, with the two figures effectively merging into one.

The motif of the combat between St George and his various human foes in some folk dramas, such as the English mummers' plays, can also be understood as a form of a pre-Christian tradition. This dramatic motif has been likened to the ancient theme of 'the two brothers', symbolizing light and dark, summer and winter: mutually dependent forces locked in a struggle where each temporary victory is merely the forerunner of temporary defeat. There is little concrete evidence to substantiate any kind of persistence of pre-Christian or extra-Christian beliefs through these plays – the simple fact of the lateness of written accounts and the post-Victorian 'revival' of folk dances and plays, with consequent questions over authenticity, must be borne in mind as a warning against too simplistic a reading. It must be admitted that the whole 'Green Man' tradition itself is beset with difficulty; nevertheless, there is some potential to understand these survivals and revivals in the context of the wide range of analogues that undoubtedly do exist, and which bring great complexity and vibrancy to the cult of this saint in many parts of the world.

The Internationalist St George

This brief survey of the analogues of St George in non-Christian traditions should give readers some sense of the extent to which this archetypal figure has permeated cultures across the globe. However, even within Christian tradition, the cult of St George is remarkable for the way in which it has spread across different countries and sects.

The origins of the cult of St George (and also Al-Khidr and Elijah) lie in the eastern Mediterranean. He is strongly associated with the Holy Land, with a tomb claimed at Lydda/Lod which is venerated by Christians and Muslims alike. The earliest references to a cult of St George occur on Syrian inscriptions dated to the mid-fourth century (just a few decades after the claimed date of his martyrdom in 303 CE), which were found during excavations at ruined churches in the nineteenth century.

There are a number of early versions of his legend, mainly from the Coptic Church;[3] the most influential of these is an apparently eyewitness account in Greek from the fifth century, which purports to have been written by a servant called Pasicrates. This character is almost certainly a convenient invention by hagiographers seeking to give a flavour of authenticity to the legend – although the fact that this very detailed account claims that the saint's torture lasted for seven years, including four executions and three resurrections, would tend to belie any claims to credibility. The key point here is that it is the story itself, and the general Christian truths it espoused, which was important to the tale tellers and their audience – what was literally true was really of little interest. There are many inconsistencies in the early legends, especially the Pasicrates version, but these are simply minor details alongside the overall purpose of encouraging devotion to the saint.

As the centuries passed more and more versions of the legend appeared, and we also see increasing amounts of evidence for a growing cult in the form of the dedication of churches to St George, inclusions of his name and feast day in lists of martyrs, and mentions in inventories of relics. Interest in him reached western Europe in the sixth century, and by the eighth century it is clear that the cult was general throughout Christian areas. A wide range of places and peoples have claimed him as their special guardian – at various times he has acted as the patron saint of Germany, Portugal, Armenia, Denmark, Hungary, Lithuania and Malta, in addition to the countries listed in the Introduction, and a large number of individual settlements are named after St George or otherwise invoke him as a patron. Thus, for example, more than 100 towns in Italy have a historic link to this saint; a number of French cities also claim his protection. Once the dragon-slaying story came to be linked with St George the extent of interest in him becomes even clearer as at least seven European countries developed localized legends.

It is against this background of a hugely popular and widespread cult that we need to understand St George's role as the patron of England. Various claims are made about when St George took on this role – the Church Council of Oxford in 1222 is sometimes said to be the key point, although they were probably more interested in fixing the date of his feast day since they deemed it to be of 'lesser rank'; the celebration of St George's Day at Windsor in 1348, which is linked to the founding of the Order of the Garter, is another date frequently cited. In 1351 there is the first record of his invocation as a patron of the English nation in battle, and in 1399 St George's feast day was officially promulgated as a festival to be observed 'as a holiday, even as other nations observe the feast of their patrons'.[4] There is ample evidence to suggest that he was very important to particular groups within English society in the late Middle Ages, especially the social elite and, above all, the monarchy. With few exceptions English kings from Edward III onwards tended to exhibit an interest in the saint through the possession of relics and the commissioning of imagery of St George, some of which presented the saint alongside the monarch himself; it is notable that St George was invoked by both sides in the Wars of the Roses – almost as if the claiming of this saint's patronage was tantamount to claiming the throne itself.

However, it was not until the eighteenth century that the saint was formally declared, by Pope Benedict XIV, as the principal protector of England. The relatively recent date of this pronouncement is often a surprise to English people, and it is fair to say that the pope was probably only regularizing a situation that had existed semi-officially for some centuries already. 'St George for Merrie England' arguably came into being as a meaningful concept in the late medieval period, mainly as a consequence of his usefulness as a symbol of authority to the monarchy and social elites. However, it was not until the post-Reformation era that we see consistent signs of construction of this saint as a native-born patron who is enmeshed in the tradition of King Arthur and the myth of Albion; it is notable that Arthurian legend, such as Thomas Malory's *Le Morte d'Arthur* (1485), experienced a dip in interest in the seventeenth century but was strongly reasserted in the Victorian period, just when the reconstruction of St George as a motif of empire was really starting to emerge.

The English Reformation could easily have signalled the end of St George's role in England. Various official sanctions were enacted against 'superstitious beliefs' – a term that included the cults of non-biblical saints – and these certainly should have encompassed the historically dubious figure of St George. However, he continued to be recognized as significant, by some sections of society at least, in the nation's conception of itself, and it is possible to trace a gradual expansion of his appeal beyond the monarchy and the social elite. Indeed, it can be argued that this reinvention of a pseudo-historical eastern Mediterranean figure as 'English of the English' was a necessary, if not deliberate, corollary of the survival and consolidation of St George as a significant figure in the cultural landscape of England after the Reformation.

It is against this broad context of variation and reimagining that St George should be approached – no one culture has a singular claim on him, and no one version of his image, legend or significance is universally applicable. With this in mind, we can now turn to consider some of the salient factors underpinning his widespread popularity.

2

Misrepresentations and Reinventions: St George across Continents and Cultures

I n many parts of the contemporary Anglophone world St George is a contested and problematic figure, but however modern-day individuals may feel about him they usually perceive a link between this saint and the concept of Englishness, a link that is also acknowledged in many of the other places and peoples which also claim him as a patron. Although we can find traces of interest in St George within England in advance of the Norman Conquest of 1066, it seems clear that his role as a cipher for the English nation has developed more recently. It is likely that the enthusiasm shown for this saint by the Pre-Raphaelite Brotherhood, and the way in which they set his character in an idealized vision of the medieval past, had a key role to play – while they did not invent the idea of St George as an Englishman, they certainly helped to cement an identification which culminated in nineteenth-century claims that he was born in Glastonbury (Somerset) or Tintagel (Cornwall): places that are infused with the Arthurian myth, and specifically the English versions of that Celtic tale.

William Morris, Dante Gabriel Rossetti, Edward Burne-Jones and their circle made a profoundly important set of contributions to the emergent modern era, not least in their beautiful artworks, their political analysis and their championing of individual skill over mechanized production. However, their singular and somewhat misguided vision of the period before the Reformation has had far-reaching consequences for the ways in which many people now think of the 'Middle Ages' – a term which is in itself a modern concept, since people living in the fourteenth and fifteenth centuries, for example, would have had no sense that they were in the 'middle' of anything other than perhaps the journey from the Creation to the Second Coming of Christ. The misunderstandings of the medieval past which are consistently trotted out in Hollywood blockbusters and television drama series can often be traced back to the door of the Pre-Raphaelites – especially the presentation of a semi-mythical world where knights errant bestrode the land rescuing swooning ladies, the ruling class spent their time alternately jousting and feasting, and everyone else (save the odd priest, friar or nun) was poor, nasty, brutish and short, as Thomas Hobbes nearly said.

These kinds of contemporary visions of the centuries before the Reformation draw heavily on the rather fey lost world conjured up by the poetry, prose and paintings of the late nineteenth century, exemplified by Morris, Rossetti and their ilk. The whimsical image they present has little grounding in reality. Where, I wonder, are their equivalents of Margaret Paston, the Norfolk gentrywoman? She wrote to her husband in the late 1450s to ask him to send her a supply of crossbows from London along with sugared almonds and dressmaking supplies, the better to allow her to arrange the defence of the family property. What about the rising merchant class with its apprentices and journeymen, the strict rules of the organizing guilds and the incipient power of civic government? Why do we never see the religious heretics of the fourteenth and fifteenth centuries, such as the Lollards, who challenged the belief system of the Roman Catholic Church and proved to be a significant influence on Martin Luther and other reformers in the sixteenth century? The Pre-Raphaelites, and those who were influenced by them, were generally not interested in this nuanced and messy version of the medieval world, preferring to view it as a lost age of perfection where valiant heroes battled evil foes, both human and monstrous, and everyone knew their place.

It is difficult to establish clear lines of influence on the Pre-Raphaelites in relation to St George, but it is likely that they were aware of post-medieval writers such as Richard Johnson, whose influential work *The Most Famous History of the Seven Champions of*

Christendom (1576–80) seems to represent the zenith (or perhaps the nadir) of the romanticization of the legend of the saint. This long and complex story went through many editions from its first publication through to the early twentieth century and inspired several imitations, such as the chapbook *The Life and Death of St George, the Noble Champion of England* (seven editions between 1750 and 1820), and the poems *The Birth of St George* and *St George and the Dragon* (published in Bishop Percy's *Reliques of Ancient English Poetry*, another very popular work which went through many editions following its initial publication in 1765). Johnson's account of St George's life is a considerable elaboration of the medieval narrative; it has little in common with the modern Coptic version outlined in the introductory chapter of this book, and it is of enormous interest as an example of the extent to which writers have been prepared to change and embellish a well-known narrative.

In Johnson's retelling our hero is born in Coventry – this may well be the first time that this eastern Mediterranean figure was recast as a native Englishman. He was kidnapped as an infant by a wicked enchantress who fell in love with him as he reached manhood, but he resisted her dubious charms, contrived to entrap her using her own magic wand, then freed the other six champions of Christendom (including St Andrew, St Patrick and St David – the patrons of the 'home nations' of Britain) that she had been holding captive, so that all could go off on glorious adventures. St George's own odyssey includes the rescue of an Egyptian princess, whom he marries and takes home to Coventry where they have three sons, one of whom grows up to be the monster-slayer Guy of Warwick. Johnson's work gives us a strong sense that he is reinventing St George as a suitable English patron in a manner to appeal to a post-Reformation English readership – the simple fact that he is constructed as a married man clearly marks out this treatment from the medieval tradition of the virginal knight errant. The popularity of the *Seven Champions* is only one example of the ongoing and developing interest in St George in the post-Reformation period: an equally elaborate, but intellectually far more challenging, version of the life of this saint is provided by Edmund Spenser in *The Faerie Queene* (1590), which also plays upon

How the good Knight St George of England slew the dragon and set the Princess Free

Dante Gabriel Rossetti, stained and painted glass panel
of St George and the dragon, *c.* 1862.

Johnson's identification of the saint as English and prone to romantic liaisons.

It is against this context of the misunderstanding and misrepresentation of the Middle Ages that we need to view the work shown here, with its clear presentation of St George as an embodiment of Englishness. Created by the firm of Morris, Marshall, Faulkner & Co. to designs by Dante Gabriel Rossetti, this stained glass panel is one of a series of six images which focus on the legend – or rather a version of the legend – of St George and the dragon. It provides us with a significant cultural model of St George in the late nineteenth century, a model that has helped to shape some of the most pervasive contemporary English understandings of the national patron. Morris & Co., founded in 1861, created stained glass for secular use, even though the imagery sometimes had a religious theme, and the panels in this series are thought to have been designed for windows at Harden Hall in Bingley, West Yorkshire. However, the firm built up an extensive collection of designs that could be reproduced or adapted for new commissions so the intended destination of this particular set, now to be found at the Victoria and Albert Museum in London, is uncertain.

The narrative presented in the panels starts with a royal couple (the inscription tells us this is the 'King of Egypt', the woman is not remarked upon) being told about the depredations of the dragon, which can only be satisfied by maidens. They are presented with a picture of the monster and a basket of skulls, presumably to emphasize the point. The imagery then proceeds through the drawing of lots and the princess being taken to her fate in a carriage. The image shown is the fourth of the six subjects in the sequence. Inscribed 'How the good Knight St George of England slew the dragon and set the Princess free', it offers several points for discussion. First, the princess is presented semi-naked: this is never seen in medieval treatments, and her nudity owes much to eighteenth- and nineteenth-century depictions of the rescue of Angélique by Roger, and the parallel rescue of Andromeda by Perseus – classical myths of dragon-slaying heroes that are near-analogues of the story of St George and the dragon, but far more romantic in nature. Second, St George has jammed his shield into the monster's mouth – this is most unmedieval – although we should note that he is also attacking the dragon's throat in the standard medieval fashion. The treatment of the dragon's tail is also likely to have been influenced by medieval imagery: the long snaky coils wrap around St George's right leg and up his torso, in an exaggerated version of the motif of the tail curled about the leg of St George's horse seen in the genuinely fifteenth-century illustration opposite. Above all, St George is described in the inscription as 'of England'. The idea of his Englishness is underlined by the pattern of St George's crosses on his surcoat, which are presented in a similar guise to the primary device used by the Order of the Garter.

The gulf which is apparent between Pre-Raphaelite understandings of the medieval legends of St George and the reality, according to the written and visual records that we have, is evident in the narrative expressed in inscriptions included in these stained glass panels, as well as the iconography itself. The other subjects in the sequence depict a story that would be deeply unfamiliar to a medieval audience – only a young unmarried woman is able to satisfy the dragon's appetite, whereas the conventional tradition claims merely that a young person (gender and sexual condition unstated) is sacrificed because the supply of sheep is running low. The sorrowing princess rides in a carriage to meet her fate – in medieval versions she walks out bravely to face the monster, and even tries to encourage St George to save himself rather than risk his life to save her. Above all, the final image shows a wedding feast for St George and the rescued princess – the possibility of this marriage is alluded to in some genuine medieval English versions of the story, with the princess's hand offered in marriage as a reward, but the chaste saint always refuses the

Statue of St George and the dragon, 15th-century polychromed wood, Coventry.

match and continues on his way, a virginal knight in the service of the Virgin Mary.[1] By contrast, this Pre-Raphaelite treatment conforms to post-medieval versions of the legend where St George marries the princess, as we find in Johnson's *Seven Champions*, and arguably helps to cement this new vision of the saint as a 'true Englishman', with a wife and home to protect.

Another aspect of a romantic vision of Englishness can be detected in the fifth panel, where St George and the princess ride to her home in a carriage and the vanquished dragon's head is borne aloft by a figure dressed as a medieval peasant, rather in the manner of a morris dancer holding up an inflated bladder on a stick. This detail may indicate that the design was influenced by springtime customs associated with St George in the post-medieval period, such as the presentation of mummers' plays and pace-eggers' plays (northern English versions of the hero-combat play, usually performed at Easter), whose actors were often involved in the performance of morris dances too. Meanwhile, this visual cycle contains no reference to the baptism of the princess, her parents and the people of the city – this is a standard motif in medieval English versions of the dragon legend – and there is no mention of the martyrdom narrative which was such a significant part of the medieval conception of St George.[2] This development tends to suggest that the concept of St George as the romantic hero, rather than the Christian martyr, had become well entrenched in English understandings of the saint by the late nineteenth century.

St George beyond England

If twentieth- and twenty-first-century understandings of St George in Britain have been shaped by the misrepresentations and allegorizations of the Pre-Raphaelites, Johnson, Spenser and other post-Reformation artists and writers, they have also been affected by a widespread conviction that interest in this saint, even if the man himself was not actually 'English' in any meaningful sense, is somehow peculiar to England. As we have already seen this is very far from the truth, since he is recognized as the patron saint of a range of countries, cities and peoples – and it is fair to say that there is no general acknowledgement of him as an Englishman anywhere outside Britain, with the possible exception of territories which have been subject to British rule. In fact, the efforts made by proponents of the English cult to claim him as native probably exemplify a broader tendency to recreate a patron saint as a local hero, with narratives set in a recognizable cultural landscape of 'home'. Thus we find stories of St George leaping on horseback from a mountain peak in Crete as he evaded his enemies – with a chapel marking the place where he safely landed – and breaking sieges in Malta and the Holy Land. He is said to have appeared to help soldiers at battles in Spain as well as at the English victory over the French at Agincourt, and allegedly manifested himself in both armies in a battle between Denmark and Sweden. If we consider the number of places where his dragon-slaying adventure is localized, the evidence for a deliberate reshaping of the story is even more stark; many western European traditions place the event in Palestine, Syria or Libya, but six sites in England claim to be the 'true' location; in the German version the battle took place at Berlin or Furth; the Dutch locate the story at Oudenaarde in East Flanders; the Wallachians at Orwoza; the Catalans at Montblanc; the Danes at Svendborg; and the Swedes at Tabiam.

St George's cult has been enthusiastically adopted even where there is no tradition of a dragon fight, and traces of it can turn up in some surprising places. A statue of the saint is located on the island of Lamb Holm in Orkney. This near-life-sized work stands outside the Italian Chapel, which was created by Italian prisoners of war from two Nissen huts in 1943–4. These men were sent to Orkney to construct the Churchill Barriers that seal off the southern end of Scapa Flow, and the chapel and its associated statue are the last remnants of Camp 60. The Italian Chapel is apparently the most visited attraction in the Orkney Islands, but accounts of the place usually fail to make any mention of the statue, which was created from barbed wire and concrete before the chapel was even started. This omission is probably because most British commentators would identify St George as 'English', and hence feel baffled by the presence of the statue on Scottish (or, more correctly, Orcadian) soil. However, it can be

Domenico Chiocchetti, *St George and the Dragon*,
1943, concrete, Lamb Holm, Orkney.

plausibly argued that St George was sufficiently meaningful to the
Italian soldiers that the artist and sculptor in their number, Domenico
Chiocchetti, created an image of him even before he was able to lead
the construction of a place of worship. This is a devotion which the
prisoners must have brought with them from home: St George is a
soldier-saint, of course, and hence of general appeal to members of the
armed forces around the world, but he is so popular in Italy that more
than a hundred communities invoke him in their name. The St George
statue was erected despite, rather than because of, any connection he
may have had to the English, indeed, the sculpture was created before
Italy capitulated to the Allies, so if the Italians had identified St
George as English they would have been highly unlikely to have
wanted to grace their camp square with his image.

A telling comment by one of the prisoners of war is recounted in
the information boards at the Italian Chapel: 'It [the statue] is the symbol of a will to "kill" all misunderstandings among people of different

cultures. As the St George was built to express the physical and psychological pain, so was the chapel conceived to meet a spiritual need.' The trend to depict St George on war memorials may also reflect this desire to encapsulate the trauma, as well as the heroism, of war: his status as a military saint is not simply a question of presenting an uncomplicated image of valour. The image below shows the very striking war memorial in Groningen, a city in the north of the Netherlands. Created by the Dutch sculptor Oswald Wenckebach and unveiled in 1959, the work shows a huge bronze St George, simply dressed in some kind of tabard rather than presented as the more traditional medieval knight depicted by Chiocchetti, and indeed by Wenckebach himself in an earlier work, the stone war memorial on the town hall of Gouda which was unveiled in 1948. The Groningen dragon is a relief carving on three sides of the stone plinth, with particularly striking curved teeth. The piece is thought-provoking since it presents the victorious soldier as wearied by the fight rather than triumphant – it perhaps

Oswald Wenckebach, *St George and the Dragon*, 1959, war memorial, bronze and stone, Groningen, Netherlands.

reflects the long road to recovery that Europe was still experiencing more than a decade after the war officially ended.

During my research for this book I visited specific St George festivities in Belgium and Georgia; I have previously witnessed celebrations in Malta and Crete as well as considerably more muted equivalents in England. I have also discussed St George with a range of people who have been able to inform me about his cult in Brazil, Ethiopia and Palestine, and I have benefitted from access to the published works of scholars who have written about devotions to the saint in Lebanon, the Setu people of the far north of Europe, the Roma of Eastern Europe and elsewhere: the discussion which follows is by no means all that could be said, but I hope it will give a flavour of the richness and vitality that characterizes the cult of St George in so many places.

St George in the Eastern Mediterranean

The likely origins of St George's cult are in the Holy Land, and it is not surprising that his narratives are particularly well developed in this locale and the surrounding areas. As we have seen, he has analogues in a number of different religions but his roles in the Abrahamic faiths, themselves focused on the Holy Land, of course, are especially striking: it is no surprise that this general area is particularly rich with stories of the saint and his power. Thus we find that people with long-term illnesses and injuries resort to the 'chains of St George', which are claimed as a relic of his imprisonment: they are kissed in an act of veneration, then wrapped around the afflicted body part. The eighteenth-century English prelate, traveller and author Richard Pococke recounted seeing an iron collar attached by a chain to a pillar in the Greek Orthodox church of St George in Cairo, which he was assured would cure psychiatric illness if the sufferer was confined in the collar for three days, and a film on YouTube uploaded in August 2009 shows what is likely to be the same collar and chain described by Pococke.[3] There are documented examples of the use of parallel relics among Palestinian Christians in the present day, for example, in the monastery church at Al-Khader – a place name that clearly invokes the Islamic analogue to St George, Al-Khidr.

In his writings, Pococke commented on the extent to which Turks were said to be devoted to St George, in what may well be a reference to Al-Khidr; it is notable that various Christian sects in the eastern Mediterranean are also strongly attached to this figure, and it may well be that cross-fertilization between different religious traditions is at work.

A good example of this trend can be found in Lebanon, where St George is venerated – as a symbol of fertility and rebirth, and also as a mounted knight – not only by Christians but by Muslims and the substantial Druze community (some of whom identify as Muslim while others claim their belief system to be essentially separate from Islam). St George is the dedicatee of 276 churches, 27 monasteries, 26 schools, two hospitals and two mosques, in addition to a number of villages, shrines and sanctuaries all over the country. His patronages include the capital city, Beirut, which has its own Bay of St George. Salih Ben Yahya, an Arab Muslim historian of the fifteenth century, relates a version of the legend of St George and the dragon set in Beirut, and Richard Pococke also comments on this tradition, though it is unclear whether what he identifies is closely aligned with Salih Ben Yahya's version, which states that it was an apparition of the saint that killed the dragon, apparently to connect with the dating of major earthquakes in 495, 501 and 551 CE, which devastated Beirut. This insistence on an intangible rather than phys- ical form of the saint as the dragon-slayer is also a link with medieval stories of St George appearing as a celestial warrior to break sieges during the Crusades and also on the battlefield.

According to Marlène Kanaan,[4] local people in Beirut say that a grotto with seven coves by the mouth of the river served as the den of the dragon; the grotto was transformed into a sanctuary dedicated to both the Virgin Mary and St George (a combination familiar to western European Christians in the late Middle Ages). St George is said to have washed his hands of the blood of the dragon in the waters of a spring next to the grotto; the waters of the spring have for many years been thought to have curative value. It was reported in the 1920s that Maronite and Armenian pilgrims tied pieces of cloth, symbolizing their wishes, to the gates of the grotto; when the wishes were granted they would come back and untie the cloths. They also stuck pebbles with saliva or mud on the walls of the grotto while making wishes.

Kanaan also writes about a church in Beirut being converted to a mosque, and subsequently being shared between Maronite and Orthodox Christian communities; it passed into Muslim control in 1661 because the Christians were not able to pay the required taxes; as a mosque it is said to have held a healing well which was thought to cure pulmonary diseases and female sterility. Richard Pococke recorded a healing ritual he witnessed at this mosque, commenting that this place was known as 'Cappadocia' to medieval writers.[5] Whether or not he is correct in this assertion, it is telling that he tries to overcome his apparent confusion about the actual location of the dragon-slaying episode by eliding a region of modern-day Turkey with Beirut.

Another legend about this site relates that a confrontation between St George and the Prophet Muhammad took place there, concerning who was most favoured by God in accomplishing miracles. The Prophet Muhammad is said to have hit the ground of the mosque with his stick in an effort to obtain water, but in vain; when St George did the same with his lance, a spring of water gushed from the ground. This story is reminiscent of the account of the meeting between Musa (Moses) and Al-Khidr, where devotees of the saint are shown that their champion is stronger than even the most lauded figures in other Abrahamic traditions.

Kanaan describes the popularity of St George in Lebanon as an 'incontestable fact'.[6] She says that his name acts as a leitmotif, with constant invocations. This seems to be summed up in the expression used as the title of the Introduction to this book, apparently derived from the Kourani people of the country: 'God is great but not like St George.' What higher accolade can be accorded to any figure?

Lebanon is, of course, geographically very close to Palestine, and it is clear that St George has an equally lively cult here. There are many facets to his devotion among Palestinians of various religious traditions, but he is particularly associated with healing and protection against political upheaval. In terms of the latter role, the village of Al-Khader has two myths which claim that he has protected the people from very specific threats. In 1948 St George appeared in the sky, saving the settlement from the worse fate which befell the villages to the immediate west, and in the Second Intifada (2000) the sound of the saint's horse could be heard, making protective sweeps around the village at night during the curfew. More physical evidence of the cult can be found in the form of a relic of St George's blood in a silver vial in the chapel dedicated to him within the monastery of Mar Saba, and chains of St George are used for healing there just as in Cairo. The Byzantine monastery in Beit Jala is known to have been dedicated to St George, although it is mainly associated with St Nicholas now, and there is also a chapel in St George's honour which is one of the oldest Arab Orthodox churches in the Holy Land; local Palestinians started using it sometime during the Ottoman era. In addition there is a very small church of St George in the Jewish Quarter of Jerusalem, maintained by the Greek Patriarchate. The Orthodox Christian communities in the villages and cities of Rameh, Ramla and Taybeh all have St George as patron of their churches.

St George is asked to assist with a wide range of health issues in Palestine, including mental illness (with which the chains of St George are meant to be particularly efficacious) and children with speaking difficulties (which may be cured by placing a key in the child's mouth, an act performed at the monastery in Beit Jala, with both Muslims and Christians availing of the ritual);[7] more general health issues are treated by anointing the affected parts of the body, and then the forehead and hands of the afflicted person, with the holy oil of St George, using the sign of the cross as the oil is applied. Sight problems also fall under his purview; my correspondent Dan Koski has informed me of a tale told to him by an elderly Muslim woman in the village, which states that during the time of the British Mandate (1922–48) a woman's sight was restored when she gave a gold necklace to the principal icon of St George in the monastery.

One further form of assistance which St George gives his supplicants in Palestine relates to people falling down wells or into deep pits, or from high buildings. Koski tells me that his wife's grand-father maintained until his dying day that St George had personally rescued him from a well, lifting him bodily out onto the ground, and the Greek Orthodox priest responsible for St George's church in Jerusalem recounts how a woman taking refreshments to builders working several storeys up tripped and fell to the ground, but was found to be unharmed. She said that St George had appeared and guided her gently down. Similar stories are told in the Palestinian Muslim community too: Al-Khidr appears in visions to injured people as they lie in hospital beds and heals them. I find it striking that there is a shared belief that St George/Al-Khidr appears in a physical form. This is not a question of someone praying to a saint and then rescuers or helpers turning up on his behalf. Rather, the depth of people's devotion is such that they can call upon their saint and he will answer in a very literal way.

Meanwhile, St George's name and image appear on a wide range of commercially produced foodstuffs found across the eastern Mediterranean, from vanilla essence and baking powder through a powdered orange drink called 'Freshoo', to 'Worcestershire-type sauce' and instant pudding mix. The St George's company of Egypt was established in 1906 by a Greek émigré called Stefanos Panagiotis Tamvakis; sadly, the company's website does not state why he named his foundation as he did, but I suspect that the popularity of St George in Greece may have been a compelling reason. I have only had the opportunity to try their falafel mix – just add water, shape into flat cakes and fry in hot oil. I half hoped it would be flavoured with dragon's blood, or otherwise redolent of the legend of the saint that the maker is named for, but it was not to be. Nevertheless, if all the products in the range are as tasty then no disservice is done to our hero.

St George in Ethiopia

Ethiopia has a fascinating and complex history, and its proximity to the Holy Land – lying just across the Red Sea – has meant that the impact of eastern Mediterranean belief systems has been very profound. Coptic Christianity flourished there from very early in the country's recorded history, with Egyptian influence on the northern and western borders of Ethiopia undoubtedly playing a role in its significance: it was not until the 1920s that the Ethiopian Church was able to assert itself meaningfully as a distinct tradition, despite a long record of attempts to negotiate an end to its subordination by the Church of Alexandria. Furthermore, the Beta Israel (the people of the House of Israel, a Jewish community formerly known as the Falasha, which translates from the Ethiopian language Amharic as 'exiles' or 'landless ones') were established in Ethiopia for many centuries, with one tradition tracing their ancestry to Menelik, the son of King Solomon and the Queen of Sheba. It is only since 1975 that the Beta Israel have been recognized as Jews by the state of Israel, and many thousands were airlifted from Ethiopia to Israel in the 1980s and the early 1990s; consequently, very few now remain in East Africa. Their belief system is distinct from Hebrew Judaism in a number of regards, due to the early date at which their supposed 'emigration' from the Holy Land took place, but it does include prophecies attributed to Elijah. The Beta Israel form of Judaism continues to leave a legacy in Ethiopia, and the great interest in St George that pertains there to this day may be attributable in part to the cultural interchanges between the Beta Israel and the Coptic Christians.

One of the clearest demonstrations of the extent of the Ethiopian cult of St George is found at Lalibela, a city in the Amhara region to the north of the country. Lalibela is of immense historical and religious importance, and was recognized by UNESCO as a World Heritage Site in 1978, in the very first listing of monuments described, under the terms of the scheme, as having outstanding universal value. The church of St George (Biete Ghiorgis in Amharic, meaning 'the House of St George') is one of eleven monolithic churches on the site which were sculpted, rather than built, in the thirteenth century. The roof of the church is pictured below: craftsmen carved downwards into red volcanic rock, initially hewing out huge blocks and then using chisels to form doorways, windows, columns, floors, roofs and so forth, apparently in an attempt to build a 'New Jerusalem' to act as a locus of pilgrimage in the wake of the Muslim capture of the actual

View of the roof of the early 13th-century rock-cut church at Lalibela, Ethiopia, dedicated to Biete Ghiorgis (St George).

Jerusalem. According to Ethiopian cultural history, Biete Ghiorgis was built because of a vision experienced by King Gebre Mesqel Lalibela of the Zagwé dynasty (a poorly documented period, one of the most obscure in Ethiopian history, which extended from about 1137 to 1270). St George and God have both been said to have appeared to the king and given instructions to sculpt the church, which seems to be the last of the churches to be created on the site; it stands slightly apart from the main complex of ten churches (some of which may originally have been royal palaces) and is connected to them by a system of trenches.

The British Museum owns a painting of the Battle of Adwa, fought between Ethiopia and Italy on 2 March 1896; the image itself was probably created in the 1940s. Emperor Menelik II is shown leading the Ethiopian armies to a famous victory over a large colonial Italian force, an event which is celebrated to this day with a national holiday and led to the recognition of Ethiopia as a beacon of independence and self-determination in many parts of Africa that were subject to European imperialism. The emperor is shown in the top left corner of the painting, wearing a crown and seated beneath a royal umbrella. His wife, Empress Taytu, appears in the bottom left, on horseback and carrying a revolver; in the centre of the painting, also on horseback, is the commander of the Ethiopian forces, Fitawrari Gabayyahu. It is conventional in Ethiopian painting to indicate the allegiances by showing the full faces of the 'good' characters while the 'bad' appear in profile. Hence the Ethiopian troops seem all to be turning their heads towards the viewer while the Italian troops are shown side on, often little more than stylized heads and guns.

Above the battle St George appears as the patron saint of Ethiopia, surrounded by a glory of red, yellow and green – the same colours flying above the Ethiopians. He is closely associated with the imperial family and its military forces and is shown here helping the Ethiopians to victory: three of his spears have fallen into the Italian lines. He seems to have bare feet, reflecting another convention of Ethiopian art whereby great horsemen are often shown with only one or two toes in the stirrup.

The presence of St George in the image probably relates to the fact that a relic of this saint was carried to the battle, and hence he is credited with assisting the Ethiopians to victory. Following their defeat Italian prisoners of war were put to work to construct the cathedral of St George in Addis Ababa, the capital of Ethiopia. They were perhaps rather less willing to help with the honouring of St George in this way than their later compatriots who actively chose to create the statue of St George in Orkney, but they seem to have made a good job of it nevertheless: an Italian tourist publication of 1938 described the cathedral as a fine example of the European interpretation of Ethiopian church design, although the building had actually been damaged by fire the previous year. The cathedral was the site of the coronation of a number of Ethiopian monarchs, including Emperor Haile Selassie on 2 November 1930; consequently, it is a place of pilgrimage for Rastafarians as well as Christians.

Although we see St George in the legend of the Battle of Adwa in a particularly military context, his image and identity are woven into the fabric of Ethiopian life in many ways. For example, there is a specific form of an elaborate cross shape which is identified as 'the cross of St George'; he is often depicted in wall paintings and icons, invoked in political cartoons and frequently appealed to for

Ethiopian girl wearing the cross of St George.

St George wall painting at Lake Tana, Ethiopia.

St George beer,
brewed in
Kombolcha,
Ethiopia.

help. The Amharic text on the label of St George beer, brewed in Kombolcha, Ethiopia, makes this point very strongly – it states that this beer is the 'everyday choice'. In the best sense St George is a quotidian saint, always at hand – perhaps this is the idea that the Kouranis of Lebanon are invoking when they claim that 'God is great but not like St George' – he is within reach and a constant source of help, but still worthy of special attention on specific dates.

St George across Europe

When we consider the cult of St George outside England one of the most striking features is that many of the places that consider him their patron – and indeed other areas where he is an important saint – make a huge effort to celebrate his feast day, far more than is usual on English soil. In some places there are special traditions which are followed on St George's Day. For example, in Bulgaria there is a range of rituals and celebrations on what is known as *Gergiovden*, encompassing the personal and familial – such as the tradition of playing on swings on the day – as well as the communal and civic. *Gergiovden* is used as a day to celebrate the Bulgarian Army – 'Bravery Day' – and the principal annual army parade formerly took place on this day. This seems to link to the identification of St George as an heroic soldier, but it also allows for an expression of national identity. In contrast to this militaristic approach, in Catalonia the feast is known as *El Día de los Amantes* ('The Day of Lovers'), so the honouring of St George (in Catalan known as 'Sant Jordi', see image opposite) is augmented by something akin to St Valentine's Day practices. There it is traditional for men to give roses to their sweethearts, while women give a book. Roses have been associated with this day since the Middle Ages – a tradition that has been revived in the English city of Leicester quite recently, with roses being handed out to shoppers in the town centre – but the idea of giving books is comparatively new. It seems that a bookseller in the 1920s realized that St George's Day coincided very neatly with the death dates of the dramatist William Shakespeare and the great Spanish writer Miguel de Cervantes (23 and 22 April 1616 respectively; Shakespeare's birth date is often given as 23 April 1564, which makes the day even more significant). The bookseller decided to promote this date as way to encourage people to buy more books: Barcelona, the main city in Catalonia, is the centre of publishing in the Spanish-speaking world. Today, Barcelona's principal street, Las Ramblas, and other places in the city see hundreds of stalls set up to sell either roses or books on 23 April. It is said that by the end of the day some 4 million roses and 400,000 books will have

Francisco Canyellas Balagueró, Sant Jordi,
patron saint of Catalonia, 1922, woodcut.

been sold: around half of the annual book sales in Catalonia take place on this feast day.

While these specific festivals are undoubtedly significant in allowing us to appreciate the level of interest in St George around the world, we should also be aware that he is often invoked in the names of commercial organizations and products as well as place names, street names and the dedications of churches. Just as 'The George and

Dragon' is a common pub name in England, he is referenced through all sorts of namings in other countries, from banks to schools to parks and even a university. Some of these namings are indirect, in that they are derived from the transference of a place name. An example of this process further afield is the St George Bank in Australia – the bank is named after the district of Sydney where it was founded – but whether naming is direct or indirect the result is the same, for the name and imagery of St George and his dragon are encoded into the visual and linguistic landscape.

Some of the most telling invocations of the saint are in food and drink. For example, in Greece there is a grape variety known as Aghiorghitiko (meaning St George's), found mainly in the Nemea region in the Peloponnese. It produces wines that are known for their deep red colour and aromatic complexity. A significant winery in Jordan produces a range of wines, from a Merlot to a Gewürztraminer, each of which invokes the saint in its name. The Portuguese cheese São Jorge is firm and pungent, reminiscent of Italian Parmesan; it is named after the island in the Azores where it is made (providing another example of transference of a place name), is crafted from raw cow's milk, aged from three to seven months, and is intended to be robust enough to withstand the rigours of long transportation. A more direct naming is found in the products made under the trade name Biscuits Saint Georges based in the west of France: one of their products is a jam-filled sandwich biscuit which is stamped with an image of a dragon!

These kinds of cultural reference points keep the saint alive in the popular imagination year round, but it is clear that he is widely celebrated on specific occasions too. The date of 23 April is the obvious one for many people, since it is St George's feast day in the Roman calendar, but Eastern European and Orthodox traditions, including the Roma, tend to mark 6 May, the equivalent date in the older Julian calendar. Meanwhile, some countries extend their interest in St George to other dates as well, as we shall see in the following accounts of my own visits to his festivals and feast days.

Celebrating St George in Belgium: Trinity Sunday

Of the St George-related events which I have experienced at first hand, the most spectacular communal celebration – and certainly the largest in terms of participants – is the annual event known as La Ducasse (or, familiarly, Le Doudou), held in Mons, Belgium.

La Ducasse takes place over an eight-day period, with the principal activities occurring on Trinity Sunday (which falls on the first Sunday after Pentecost in the Western tradition of Christianity, so eight weeks after Easter). A huge procession, involving thousands of participants dressed in quasi-medieval costumes accompanying a wide variety of reliquaries and religious images, wends its way through the city among crowds of spectators, many of whom wear red and white, the colours of Mons, in honour of the occasion. The festivities are theoretically focused around the procession of the relics of the local patron, St Waudru. With the exception of her head (which has its own specific reliquary), her bodily remains are housed in a large golden chapel-shaped shrine, which is formally handed over to the city on the night before the main procession in a splendid ceremony in the church dedicated to her. The next morning, Trinity Sunday, the shrine forms the focal point, carried in the *Car d'Or* (carriage of gold), an open, stunningly rococo, horse-drawn conveyance which dates from 1780.

The procession is undoubtedly very splendid, but the celebrations reach their clear apogee with a re-enactment of the combat between St George and the dragon, a pageant known by the rather convoluted title *la combat dit 'Lumeçon'* ('the combat called "*Lumeçon*"' – an apparently untranslatable word which derives from an old French term for a spectacle involving horses making circular movements), or alternatively *le jeu de Saint Georges* (the play, or game, of St George). Many spectators spend the entire morning in the Grand Place, the city's impressive main square, to ensure they have the best view possible. Certainly those who wish to try to draw hairs from the dragon's tail – much prized as lucky charms – need to be in position well before the combat begins.

La Ducasse dates back to October 1349, when relics of St Waudru and St Vincent were displayed and processed in Mons and nearby

Leafmen at La Ducasse, Mons, Belgium.

Soignies in an attempt to avoid the Black Death – the particularly virulent occurrence of the plague that swept across Europe in the late 1340s – along with various Masses in honour of the Trinity. The festival was deemed to be a success and it soon became an annual event, albeit moved to Trinity Sunday in order to avoid the capricious autumn weather. In 1380 a confraternity devoted to 'Dieu et Monseigneur saint Georges'[8] was founded in Mons by Guillaume d'Ostrevent, who was to become the count of Hainault; as with guilds of St George in late medieval England the membership was composed of the nobility and the bourgeoisie. An annual feast on 23 April was initiated, but more significantly the confraternity soon came to be involved in La Ducasse, with St George's relics being processed alongside those of St Waudru and a staging of a battle between St George and the dragon forming a dramatic interlude. From the early nineteenth century the combat was divided out from the procession and held as a separate event in the Grand Place once St Waudru's relics had been ceremonially returned to their church. The narrative employed was based closely on the version of the dragon legend popularized by the *Golden Legend*, a well-known thirteenth-century compendium of the lives of the saints, but augmented by a local legend where, in 1133, a local nobleman known as Gilles de Chin fought a monster which lived in a marsh at Wasmes. The most obvious echo of this story in La Ducasse is the role of the *chinchins*, allies of St George who battle with demons while he fights the dragon. These characters are a relatively recent but very popular addition to the combat, and the extent to which the essential narrative has been augmented over time by additional characters and new technology is indicative of the extent to which this is a lively and adaptable expression of a saint cult.

St George is invoked in Mons on a date that can be removed from his feast day by several weeks.[9] This underlines the fact that he has been grafted onto something pre-existing. Presumably the opportunity to stage a spectacular dragon fight, in the name of safeguarding the city, was just too good to miss, and La Ducasse is undoubtedly enriched by the inclusion of the saint and his coterie. Admittedly, the presence of relics of St George will have been a contributing factor to his inclusion in the ceremonial, but it should be noted that these relics are only a few among many that are processed in the grand parade with the *Car d'Or*. Indeed, the church in Mons which houses St George's relics is dedicated to St Elizabeth rather than St George himself – this would tend to emphasize that La Ducasse makes use of St George because he lends himself to public ceremony, rather than because he is particularly important as a patron of the city. However, a significant link is made between the two main elements of the ritual: the men who control the body of the dragon during the combat also have the responsibility of carrying the shrine of St Waudru from its usual position in the patronal church and placing it in the *Car d'Or*, and also for returning it back after the triumphal ascent of the *Car* up a steep incline known as the Ramp of St Waudru – this must be achieved by dray horses pulling the carriage, and their human supporters, in a single movement in order to avert disaster from the city. The actor portraying St George in the combat takes the lead in the procession at this significant moment, riding his horse through the crowds which line the ramp and clearing the way for St Waudru, immediately before he rides off to confront the dragon in the Grand Place.

It is clear that La Ducasse, and especially the combat, are deeply significant in Mons's civic identify. For example, a large image in painted tiles decorates the interior of the central railway station, invoking St Waudru but dominated by a depiction of St George overcoming the dragon; this motif is flanked by some of the characters who take part in the re-enactment. The removal of the shrine of St Waudru onto the *Car d'Or*, its procession around the city and the crucial moment of its return home are ostensibly the focus of La Ducasse, but it is evident that the episode of St George and the dragon has come to occupy the most anticipated place in the celebration. There are lots of rules about who can take part in the combat – with length of residence in the city as crucial as physical fitness – and some competition for the honour. It is clear that the cast of characters has been considerably extended over time as the performance has evolved, perhaps in part to allow greater opportunity for participation as well as to increase the element of spectacle.

St George rides a very well-trained horse (a black horse in 2012, though it is unclear whether this was a deliberate evocation of some classic Greek and Italian iconography of the saint, or merely a lucky coincidence); he wears a striking golden parade helmet with a long black mane and a yellow surcoat, with no sign of the red-and-white device that is so commonly associated with him. I found this rather surprising given the preponderance of these colours in the flags, bunting, clothing and decorations which feature in association with the event, but the use of red and white is apparently a simple reference to the communal symbolism of Mons (their flag is three vertical blocks of colour, red on either side of white). St George as presented in the combat certainly looks quite unlike the conventional portrayal of the mounted chivalric knight – underlined by the fact that his conventional sword and lance are augmented towards the end of the pageant by a most unmedieval pistol!

St George's opponent is currently a large carbon fibre model of a dragon, more than 10 metres long and weighing around 180 kg (400 lb). In previous incarnations it has been rather smaller, and carried by people sited within the body of the beast, but it is now operated by means of external handles. The dragon is controlled by two teams of costumed men – the eleven *hommes blancs*, or white men, who are in charge of the monster's body, and the eight *feuillettes*, or leaf men, who look after the tail. The most striking feature of the dragon is its enormously long tail – it is at least 8 metres (26 ft) in length, and has a number of horses' tails attached to its end. The dragon's tail plays a crucial part in the action, for it is repeatedly dropped down into the boisterous crowd which surround the combat arena.

Besides the white men and the leaf men, the dragon is assisted by eleven demons, dressed in black costumes with red horns, each carrying an inflated bladder on a stick. Their primary role is to fight the *chinchins*. They are dressed in pantomime-style tartan costumes, with a stylized horse's body attached to their own with braces. In addition, a team of policemen and firemen adds to the commotion.

La Ducasse, video screen showing St George
shooting the dragon, Mons, Belgium.

These faux-officials play an important role in holding back, and indeed physically interacting with, the crowds when the dragon's tail is threatened with destruction, and seem to be a development from the concept of a local militia. The choreographed performance lasts for around 45 minutes, with a lively and martial atmosphere maintained throughout by a loud military band, lodged on a bandstand immediately above the combat arena. The cacophony is enhanced by regular ear-splitting reports of firecrackers, presumably timed to coincide with St George's pistol shots.

There is no rescue of a maiden in the Mons version of the dragon story, perhaps in recognition of the legend of the local hero Gilles de Chin, though two female characters have played a significant role in the combat since their introduction at the start of the new millennium. The first is known as Cybèle. Dressed in yellow and black, she represents the origins of the city of Mons. She passes a lance to St George then collects the head of the weapon as he breaks it across the tail of the dragon, and gives it to lucky members of the crowd as a trophy. The second woman is known as Poliade. She represents the contemporary city; dressed in red and brown, she brings forth the pistol that will be used to deliver the *coup de grâce*. As any right-thinking member of the public would, she passes the gun to a 'policeman', who in turn gives it to St George. Poliade is also responsible for collecting the second lance used by St George, the one that does not (or should not) break.

In 2008 UNESCO designated the processional figures of giants and dragons in Belgium and France, including the dragon of La Ducasse, as a Masterpiece of the Oral and Intangible Heritage of Humanity, alongside a range of practices such as Japanese Nogaku theatre (of which Noh is the best-known form) and Ramlila, which is a performance of the Ramayana epic in India. I would certainly recommend a visit to Mons to experience La Ducasse, though perhaps not for anyone who finds large crowds to be problematic: a Belgian newspaper previewing the event claimed that 200,000 people were expected to attend the event. In reality I suspect that the numbers were somewhat lower than this in 2012, due to the inclement weather, but there was still a tremendous atmosphere throughout the whole day.

The claim made by the official guide to the event that there were to be 1,700 participants was certainly credible – the procession of the *Car d'Or* took at least an hour to pass by each location.

St George's Day in Georgia: 23 November

The celebration of St George in the Black Sea state of Georgia is a very different experience. In contrast to the large-scale communal activity in Mons, which is a significant event in the tourism calendar of the Belgian summer, celebrations in Tbilisi, the capital city, are much more low key and less obviously organized, albeit they seem to represent a very profound devotion within the Georgian Orthodox tradition. St George is one of the most important saints in Eastern Orthodox Christianity, the distinct strand of belief followed in much of Eastern Europe and the diaspora of these communities, separate from both Roman Catholicism and the Protestant churches. His feast day is usually celebrated on 6 May rather than 23 April in the Eastern Orthodox Church, due to variations with the calendar followed by Western traditions.

Broadly speaking, in Eastern Orthodox traditions the April or May feast of St George forms one of the most significant dates in the annual religious calendar, and a number of the rituals and practices associated with it are strongly linked into the saint's association with springtime and fertility. That said, although the Georgian Orthodox Church certainly keeps the spring feast of St George, it seems to be less significant than 23 November, which is identified as the feast of the translation of his relics. This choice of date seems peculiar to the Georgians, for the translation of the relics of St George is usually celebrated on 3 November – the 'translation' in question relates to a narrative of the relocation of his relics, which are said to have been taken from Nicomedia, where he is reputed to have been martyred, to Lydda/Lod in the Holy Land, where he is said to have been born. It is sometimes claimed that the November feast is kept as a reflection of the fact that Easter can overshadow the spring date, but I sense that the saint's importance may be more compelling – he is worth celebrating twice a year!

Georgia is a fascinating country, and little known in the Western world. It claims to be the originator of viticulture, and Georgian wine was certainly in great demand during the Soviet era, with much of its production being taken to Moscow. The history of the country is little short of hair-raising, with almost every 'medieval' stereotype coming to the fore at some point – episodes where a nobleman trades his mother for a horse, a duke is strangled when he steps outside to relieve himself, and a brother poisons his brother in pursuit of political power or vengeance were occurring even in the seventeenth century.[10] So it was with some element of trepidation that I visited Tbilisi, the capital city of Georgia, in November 2012, in hopes of witnessing some St George celebrations. While I singularly failed to find out any useful information before I travelled – even in the internet age I could establish little more than the fact of 23 November being a public holiday and a claim that sheep are taken to church to be blessed – and once there found that scarcely any fuller information was made available to tourists, I was not disappointed. My error was perhaps to assume that there would be some kind of special focus on the day – perhaps a civic procession or concert – but the reality was that devotion to St George is so enmeshed into the fabric of Georgian experience, and especially the life of the Georgian Orthodox Church, that the activities which mark the day are normalized. The only 'special' event I could find any reference to was a performance of a St George pantomime at the Georgian National Pantomime Theatre – a building which, it transpired, was locked up and in total darkness when I arrived for the show, despite the advertising of the performance on the wall outside. A passer-by I asked for help seemed quite unsurprised that the advertised show was not happening – perhaps reflecting an understanding that the publication of a bill of forthcoming attractions amounts to an aspiration rather than a formal undertaking to deliver.

Most British people – whether Christian or not – will mark Christmas with a special meal, a decorated tree, presents and a lot of watching of television, but I think many of us would be surprised at an anthropologist or historian coming to study these practices – to us they are just 'normal'. In the same way, many Georgians will go to church, ask for blessings, offer prayers and candles, and kiss, touch or otherwise interact with icons of St George on his feast day, but I do not think that they would necessarily identify this as a 'special' event that would be of interest to an outsider – it was all simply 'what we do' and 'normal'.

I chanced to be staying close to Kashveti Church, which is dedicated to St George, on Rustaveli Avenue, one of Tbilisi's main streets. The current Kashveti Church dates to around 1904–10 but it is a rebuilding of a much earlier edifice, with a church said to have been located here since the sixth century. Georgia boasts that it has one of the oldest Christian traditions in the world, with evidence indicating that conversion started in around 300 CE; an unbroken succession of archbishops can be traced back to 335 CE. Although even the first Kashveti Church is probably from a much later period, there is still a sense that it represents a very strong link in an immensely long chain of belief and devotion. The church is particularly celebrated for wall paintings created in 1947 by the influential Georgian artist Lado Gudiashvili, a commission that apparently led to his expulsion from the Communist Party and being fired from his teaching post at the Tbilisi Academy of Fine Arts: images of St George decorate the internal walls of the portico at the west entrance.

I was aware that many non-Protestant traditions of Christianity focus on the eve of a feast day, so after supper on the evening of 22 November I made my way to the church. The precincts and the building itself, which has a crypt chapel underneath the main vessel, were very busy, with many people standing or milling about – there are no pews anywhere in the church, so there is relative freedom of movement in the areas in front of the iconostasis, or image wall, which divides off the holiest part of the church where the altar is. I observed people wandering between the crypt and the main body of the church, which are joined by an external staircase. Many people were kissing icons; in common with most Eastern Orthodox churches there are a large number of icons, kept mostly under glass, and, although Christ, the Virgin Mary and other saints were also represented, I can safely say that I had never before seen so many images of St George in one place. The crypt in particular seemed to have very little bare space on its walls. I also noticed some people kissing the outside of the building. One layman had brought an icon of St George to be blessed by a senior priest. This process included whisking the image with holy water.

There were lots of lit candles in the church, both placed before images and also held by people – the atmosphere was very warm, both literally and figuratively, and the candle sellers were carrying on a brisk trade outside the church. A procession of clergy led to the lighting of a large candelabrum beyond the iconostasis (the doors in the centre of the image screen were left open so that we could see what was happening) and a candle was processed around the interior of the church.

The sense of warmth and colour was added to by the sound of a bell tolling in the bell tower which stands at a slight distance from the church, and some wonderful close-harmony singing from the small, all-male choir. There was some use of call-and-response with the officiating clergy, with members of the congregation joining in alongside the choir. This underlined an impression that the liturgy for St George was well known and popular. Quite a range of ages was represented. There were not many children, but certainly young people were present, including a bevy of altar boys all in red cassocks. All the women and girls present had their heads covered, usually with a scarf or shawl but also some hats, although there was little sense that anyone had dressed up in their best clothes – again, this all felt very 'normal'.

On the following morning, St George's Day itself, I went back to the church, more than half expecting to find that it was deserted. I was delighted to find that this was very far from the case – there seemed to be three times as many people there as on the previous evening, including many more children, and the atmosphere in the crypt was quite stifling thanks to the close-pressed bodies, the candles and the incense. I did manage to make my way inside and gradually through the crowd to stand near the choir, whom I had heard but not seen the previous evening. I was struck by the fact that, other than a member of the clergy in their ranks, the men were all dressed in ordinary clothes with no surplice or other obvious marker of their status in the church.

Lado Gudiashvili, St George frescoes, 1947,
Kashveti Church, Tbilisi, Georgia.

The events were similar to the previous day, but the liturgy was augmented by a large procession around the outside of building, led by clergy bearing significant objects such as processional banners and crosses, plus what seemed to be a copy of the Gospels in an ornate metal cover. Even more strikingly, especially for someone from England whose only experience of livestock in a church is the occasional Christmas or Palm Sunday donkey, was the presence of a number of cockerels and a sheep. These creatures did not form part of the official parade, but were processed around the church privately by their owners, in as much as the cockerels were carried and the sheep was dragged by main force. I asked one of the women who was holding a cockerel about the practice, and she told me that the cockerel needs to be paraded, or carried, round the church three times in order to obtain blessings for its future health and fertility. She assured me that the cockerel was not destined for the cooking pot! One cockerel-carrier that I observed stopped at each side of the church for a moment and crossed herself (though I noted that she was not obviously blessing the cockerel). I saw no sign of the recalcitrant sheep being actively blessed – though in the crush of people I may have missed it – but I sensed that it was the act of making a circumlocution of the building that provided the blessing rather than any gesticulation over the animal. However, I did see much blessing of people, carried out by senior priests in particularly splendid robes. Whisking of holy water was a popular feature, with people lifting their hands to the falling water, and also blessing by laying a hand on the supplicant's head. Another aspect of the celebration was that a large number of small cakes or bread rolls, stamped with holy symbols on top, were in evidence – in some cases they seemed to be offerings to the saint, since many were left before icons of St George on top of handwritten notes, possibly prayers, but I also saw people taking the cakes away or eating them on the spot. This is perhaps an equivalent of the distribution of blessed bread flavoured with caraway that I had previously witnessed as part of a St George celebration in Crete (described below).

There was a lot of activity at an external icon of St George which was decorated with fresh flowers. By now I was used to seeing ranks of candles before images, with a stream of people adding freshly lit ones, but this was the first time that I noted recitations being given by young boys. Unfortunately I was unable to establish what was being recited, but it was clearly a source of pride to family members as many photographs and videos were being taken.

However, I was able to pick out the many mentions of St George's name in the liturgy which was being enacted inside the church; it seemed to be a Mass, since I saw a covered chalice although I did not observe anyone receiving Communion, either bread or wine. As with the previous evening the large bell tolled in the belfry, especially to accompany the main procession, and there were also small bells rung as part of the blessing given by senior clergy standing before the iconostasis. I was struck by the fact that I did not see any photography within the church – this was very different to what I had previously witnessed in Gozo (especially when the St George statue was being removed from its niche and processed out of the church, discussed below) and in Belgium (when the reliquary of St Waudru was being ceremonially handed over to the city, everyone seemed to want their

Sheep reluctant to join the procession on St George's Day
at Kashveti Church, Tbilisi, Georgia.

Cockerel in the St George's Day procession at Kashveti Church, Tbilisi, Georgia.

own record of the event). Again, perhaps this underlines the sense I had that the Georgians experienced the St George feast day as 'special' but also 'normal', part of the cycle of the year and not necessarily something to be immortalized every time it happened.

While in Tbilisi I also visited an Armenian cathedral dedicated to St George and observed a large silver icon of the saint, alongside an icon of Christ, set out on a prayer desk in the middle of the nave, presumably as a marker of the significant date and to allow devotees to have easy access to the icon. Something similar seemed to be happening in the Georgian Orthodox Kashveti Church, though because of the press of people I could not get close enough to the prayer desk to see exactly what was on it. A visit to the city's main Orthodox cathedral a couple of days after the feast showed that worshippers were still paying particular attention to icons of the saint. The frame of a large image was decked with flowers, and banks of candles were lit in front of it, with devotees touching and kissing the glass covering the icon, praying before it and crossing themselves, much as I had seen in the Kashveti Church; the impression I had was that although the main focus of the feast had been on 23 November, its influence spread into the surrounding days, though I would not be surprised to find devotees before the icon of St George at any time of year, such is his place in Georgian consciousness. I noted that his image was one of the most frequently found in the many icon shops that Tbilisi has, and a visit to the Museum of Soviet Occupation demonstrated that a motif of the saint appeared on the Declaration of Independence of Georgia from 1918 and also the Act of Restoration of State Independence of 1991. The consistency with which he is invoked, both in terms of national identity and personal devotion, speaks volumes about the very special place he occupies in Georgian consciousness.

St George's Day in Gozo: The Week of 23 April

Like Georgia, Gozo – the second largest island in the archipelago that forms the Mediterranean country of Malta – has two St George festivals a year. They mark the feast day of their patron saint on 23 April, and then have a second festival based around the third Sunday in July – although the entire event lasts for three weeks. The significance of the July date is somewhat obscure, but a reasonable explanation seems to be that summer weather tends to be better for the pageants, horse racing and fireworks that take place.

My own experience of the Gozo festivities was in April 2003, when I was invited to speak at a conference marking 1,700 years since the generally agreed date of St George's martyrdom (303 CE) – the anniversary was observed in various ways in Malta, including the issuing of commemorative postage stamps featuring images of St George displayed in churches and chapels. The enthusiasm for marking the seventeenth centenary was in stark contrast to the English reaction to this auspicious date, which was, apparently, so lukewarm as to be non-existent.

During my week on Gozo I witnessed a number of ceremonies in the island's main town, Rabat (also known as Victoria), including a special Mass that featured the display and veneration of a relic of the saint, a panegyric (an oration about the saint's life, his Christian heroism and his power of intercession) and the celebration of liturgies in his honour. However, the most striking element for me was the huge excitement around the removal of the life-size wooden statue of St George from its niche in the basilica dedicated to him and its shoulder-high parading around part of the town before its installation on a plinth of honour for the duration of the celebrations. The statue is extremely heavy: a team of strong men is required to carry it on a special platform equipped with spars which stick out on opposite sides to allow the men to carry it almost like pallbearers. An emotional and voluble crowd greeted the statue at every stage of its journey, and the flashes from mobile phones, both within and outside the basilica, told us that many people were photographing the statue so that images could be transmitted to devotees who were unable to be present – some of whom were clearly the recipients of running commentaries given over the same phones.

While I have not personally witnessed the summer celebrations I am assured that they are filled with colour and sound, with choirs, bands and, of course, processions. The statue of St George that is paraded and venerated with such enthusiasm in Rabat is the work of a nineteenth-century Maltese sculptor, Pietro Paolo Azzopardi (1791–1875). The sculpture shows a relatively adolescent George wearing a Roman centurion's tunic and helmet, gazing towards heaven; the figure holds a palm frond, to signify his status as a martyr, in his left hand; the right hand is open, apparently to invite prayers of intercession. Although a sword hangs from his girdle and a small dragon lies under his left foot, the emphasis is on the saint as a heavenly intercessor rather an earthly warrior. The polychromed image was crafted from a mulberry trunk on the main island of Malta, and brought to Gozo sometime before 1839. There are two traditions to explain the sculpture's presence on Gozo. First, it may have been commissioned as a thank-offering by a local wealthy family for a recovery from serious illness following prayers to St George; alternatively, it may have been presented to the basilica as a gift from the parish priest in fulfilment of a vow made to the saint when he was appealed to for protection against a cholera epidemic, which was sweeping the islands in 1837.

There is a strong and popular tradition of parading a number of life-size statues of St George during the July festivities in particular; other statues are paraded for other festivals, and the team of statue carriers develop a characteristic lump of muscle on the shoulder that bears the weight of the image – it is a source of much pride, and indicates devotion both to the saint and also, I sense, to the service of the local community. Furthermore, the carriers have a special method of walking, almost like a dance step, which they reserve for carrying the St George image. This elaboration serves to underline the saint's significance as a patron of Gozo – he is often referred to as the protector of the Gozitan people.

St George's Day in Crete: 23 April

My first experience of a large-scale celebration of St George was in Crete, the largest island in the Greek archipelago, which I happened to be visiting in April 1999. I was aware that St George's Day would fall during my time on the island, and had a limited sense of the popularity of St George's cult in Greece, but little expectation that any kind of festivity would be taking place – indication, if any were needed, of the extent to which St George's international cult is a mystery to most English people. I had sought out a local English person in hopes that she might be able to direct me to a particular church or chapel for a special service or ceremony, but I was told that nothing much would happen other than that men and boys bearing the name George and its variants would be given presents by family and friends. How wrong this was: purely by chance I found that the feast day was celebrated with considerable fervour.

I happened to be staying quite near a monastery dedicated to St George outside Sissi, in the east of the island, and as I made a personal pilgrimage to the chapel there I realized that a large market specializing in toys (perhaps in reflection of St George's iden-tification as a patron of youth) was taking place outside its gates. As I drew closer it became apparent that many hundreds of pilgrims had arrived to attend a special service for the feast day, which was held in the monastery's chapel and relayed on loudspeakers to the huge crowds outside. Penitents came on their knees, and votive offerings were made: the saint was being appealed to for help and also thanked for his intercession. Large loaves of bread made with caraway seeds were blessed, broken up and distributed, along with small printed images of the saint. Bells were rung, and a large metal bar suspended from the ceiling of a room near the chapel was beaten with hammers to add to the cacophony. I have since discovered that on St George's Day services are held at many chapels and churches dedicated to the saint, and outdoor feasts – often featuring roast lamb – frequently follow. At Asi Gonia Apokoronou, near Rethymno in the central part of Crete, hundreds of shepherds bring their sheep to be blessed by priests on St George's Day. They hope to receive the protection of the saint, to ensure healthy flocks and a prosperous year.

This closing thought underlines the significance of St George as a protector of domestic animals and a harbinger of springtime – something that is largely forgotten in the English understanding of this saint. As we shall see in the next chapter, this element forms a significant focus of his wider cult.

3

St George and the Natural World:
A Symbol of Fertility

Here's one, two three jolly lads all in one mind
We've come a pace-egging and I hope you'll prove kind
An' I hope you'll prove kind, with your eggs and strong beer
And we'll come no more nigh you until the next year.

These words open the *Bury Pace-egging Play* as recorded in the autobiography, published in 1949, of J. Barlow Brooks, a Lancashire mill lad who became a Methodist minister.[1] The reference to 'pace' indicates that the play is performed at Eastertide – 'pace' is a form of 'pasch' and 'paschal', terms that allude to Christ's 'Passion' at Easter and are ultimately derived from the Hebrew *Pesach*, or Passover, the Jewish holiday which is strongly associated with the origins and dating of the Christian festival of Easter. This pace-egging play is part of the canon of traditional dramatic performances known as mumming plays, which are found in many parts of England and to a limited extent in Wales, southern Scotland and on the Isle of Man. St George is the most common character to occur in mumming plays, especially the form known as the hero-combat, which occurs far more frequently than other genres such as the sword play and the wooing play. In many places mumming plays are performed at Christmas or New Year, but Lancashire and some other parts of northwest England associated mumming with Eastertime. This fits perfectly with the evidence, widespread across Europe, that links St George with springtime rituals and festivities.

Another version of this play, which goes by a variant title of *The Peace Egg*, was recorded in a publication of around 1840 by the printer Joseph Wrigley of Manchester – a city that is still considered to be part of Lancashire by anyone who does not give too much regard to the reorganization of local government boundaries carried out in 1974. The opening stanza makes reference to 'Christmas time', which seems to indicate that it is part of a tradition that links pace-egging to New Year or Plough Monday (the first Monday after Twelfth Night, so usually towards the middle of January), although Easter is the most usual festival to which the plays are linked – indeed, the Bury text makes specific reference to 'this 'appy Easter time'. It could be that *The Peace Egg* was influenced by the practices of places outside the northwest; it is very hard to clarify the extent to which written texts are faithful to the original conception, especially because there is inevitably scant authority on which securely to discuss the oral tradition from which the textual tradition has developed. There is very little evidence for performances of mummers' plays before 1750, and it is worth remembering that modern versions of these plays that feature a scene of St George fighting a dragon tend to have little connection to older texts.

St George enters in the second stanza of the *The Peace Egg*. His speech begins:

I am St George, who from old England sprung,
My famous name throughout the world hath run.
Many bloody deeds and wonders I have made known,
And made the tyrants tremble on their throne.

The claiming of the saint as English by birth clearly identifies this as a post-Reformation tradition; it is often said that Richard Johnson's *Seven Champions of Christendom* (1576–80) is a strong influence on the presentation of St George in the mumming tradition, especially through the dramatization published by John Kirke in 1638,[2] and this Englishing of him certainly fits with Johnson's approach. However, that is not to say that the earlier traditions are entirely lost. One striking point about the mumming St George is that he fights only human enemies, characters who bear names such as Bold Slasher, the Black Prince of Paradine/Paradise and the Turkish Knight. The combat with the dragon is often referred to in his speeches, but it is never presented as the subject of the drama. This is not because a dragon would be difficult to portray on stage: the evidence of late medieval Ridings (processions) of St George, which even extends to telling us that gunpowder was used in the Norwich dragon in 1489, indicates that a dragon could be depicted if required. Indeed, dragon-like monsters were also seen in mystery plays such as the Harrowing of Hell. Rather, the emphasis seems to have been on the older and – for the late Middle Ages – parallel tradition of St George triumphing over human foes, as found in stories and imagery of St George leading armies into battle (during the Crusades and at Agincourt, for example) or the late medieval English tradition of St George as the champion of the Virgin Mary.[3] In this narrative he is overcome by his foes, captured and executed, but then resurrected by the Virgin and armed as her champion. The same motif of healing – if not actual raising from the dead – is found in the mumming plays, with St George, and sometimes one or more of his enemies, healed by a doctor.

There is a lot of controversy about what mumming plays actually mean. The most popular theory – albeit one that is based on supposition rather than hard evidence – is that they are a relic of a pre-Christian ritual relating to fertility, with a kind of sympathetic magic being deployed to ensure the return of the sun. This reading, insecure though it is, certainly does work for a Christmastide performance, for Christmas is, of course, very close to the winter solstice, when days start to lengthen again – but to my mind it is even more applicable at Eastertide, when the earth is usually starting to warm up, the sap is rising and seeds planted before the winter are beginning to sprout. Certainly, St George is commonly linked with this time of year elsewhere in Europe, and the fact that his feast day falls on 23 April is no coincidence in this regard.

Some fascinating work by the Estonian folklorist Mall Hiiemäe has helped to bring to light the range of customs and traditions that link St George to springtime, and agriculture in particular, in northern and central Europe, most of which were recorded during the nineteenth and twentieth centuries.[4] Hiiemäe notes that nearly one-third of springtime traditions in the Estonian calendar relate to St George's Day (known as *jüripäev*): this underlines the significance of the saint as well as his connection to agriculture and the fertility of both the land and animals. In some areas, especially the Baltic provinces,

St George's Day (23 April, or 6 May in the older Julian calendar) was used as the date when contracts were started and when taxes were due, so the date was significant for economic reasons too.

Besides the date of his feast day, the key starting point for the connection between St George and agriculture is the origin of his name. The Greek form *Georgios* means a ploughman, a cultivator of land, and a number of proverbs cited by Hiiemäe play very clearly on this concept. Hence the Russian sayings 'George will bring spring' and 'There is no spring without George'; in Lithuanian tradition the saint is addressed as the keeper of the keys of summer and asked to make the grass grow and to disperse the clouds. A Russian proverb states 'When George comes, the plough will go to the field'; in Finland the comparable saying is 'George will take the plough to the field'. In many places it is forbidden, or at least inadvisable, to sit or lie on the ground before St George's Day, when nature is thought to awake. In some places the earth is thought to be actively poisonous before the feast day. In Estonia walking barefoot before St George's Day could cause skin diseases, swellings and cracked skin, and among eastern Slavs there are records of beliefs that morning dew is dangerous before, or on, St George's Day as the earth is filled with poison.

Although St George's name connects him to agriculture in general, his depiction as a mounted knight links him to horses in particular, and he is recognized as a patron of horses in many locations, including Germany, Hungary, Poland, Russia, Latvia and Estonia. The association was also made in medieval England, where evidence survives of a charm invoking St George which was used to protect horses against the nightmare. Today we use this term to mean bad dreams, but for medieval people a nightmare was an evil spirit who caused bad dreams (despite the element 'mare' in the name, which brings to mind a female horse, the terms are unrelated, and the spirit took on a human form, especially that of an old woman). The nightmare hag would sit on the stomach or chest of the sleeper and send bad dreams into them, and she would also ride horses throughout the night so that when their owners needed them in the morning they would be exhausted. Hence the need for a charm to keep her away from your stable – and who better to invoke than St George. The following words should be written on a piece of parchment, which is rolled up and pushed through a stone with a natural hole in it; the stone is then suspended in the horse's mane or within the stable – perhaps in order to protect a number of horses housed together.

In nomine Patris, etc.

Saint Jorge, our Lady Knight,
He walked day, he walked night,
Til that he founde that foule wight;
And when that he her founde,
He her bete and he her bounde,
Till trewly ther her trowth she plight
That she sholde not come by night
Within seven rod of lande space
Theras Saint Jeorge y-named was.
St Jeorge, St Jeorge, St Jeorge

In nomine Patris, etc.[5]

The invocation here of St George as 'our Lady['s] Knight' relates to the story of his resurrection by the Virgin Mary and arming as her champion. Although a strong link between St George and the Virgin Mary is found in various places in Europe, the narrative from which this particular nomenclature derives does seem to be specifically English, so we can be confident that this charm arose within an English context, and it may well be indicative of a more general association between St George and the welfare of horses in the country. If this inference is correct, it certainly sets England within a strong European tradition. One Welsh example of the link is the existence of a healing well in the hamlet of St George, also known as Llan Sain Siôr (historically Denbighshire, now Conwy). The water is reputed to cure or protect horses from disease – it was claimed to be so efficacious that a whole stable of horses could experience the benefits if just one of their number drank water drawn from the well.

Although the special link between St George and horses may be largely missing from modern British understandings of the saint (other than the tendency to depict him on horseback), there is plenty of evidence for this patronage elsewhere in Europe during the twentieth century. Hiiemäe cites an interview recorded with a member of the Setu people of south Estonia in the early 1970s which includes an explanation of why (in common with Georgia) the saint has two feast days there, one in April and one in November:

> It's St George's Day; he is the animals' patron too. A beast came out of the sea and every day a human was given and then the princess was to go. She cried very pitifully. And then came St George on a white horse. St George drove a lance down the beast's throat. So God gave him two holidays for saving the people. In Värska there is St George's Church. The horses were all taken to the church to be whisked with holy water.

An earlier recording, from 1942, has another Setu speaker relating that:

> On St George's Day the horses were taken to the church and unharnessed. There were horses from every village. They were gathered on an open place. There the priest burned incense and blessed them. There was a pail with water and a whisk in it, with that whisk he threw water at the horses and said: 'Saint George, keep the horses from misfortune.' An icon with St George was also in his hand. Then the people said: 'Now the horses are blessed.' Everybody had his herdchildren also along at church. The herdchildren stood all near the priest. Then the priest blessed them so that St George would let everybody live in peace, people as well as the animals.

The Setu are claimed as the oldest settled people in Europe, with a rich oral cultural heritage: some of the songs they still sing are thought to be more than 5,000 years old. The fact that St George is important to them as the patron of horses, and indeed domesticated animals more generally, may be indicative of a wider tradition that has been lost from some places in modern times. However, the custom of honouring horses on St George's Day is found quite widely in Europe: horses are encouraged to swim on 23 April in parts of Estonia, Russia and Latvia, for example. Setu evidence from 1940 tells us of cattle and other domestic animals being blessed as well as horses. Images, including those of St George and St Nicholas, were carried around the cattle, and the animals as well as the herdchildren were whisked with holy water, and the animals were hit with willows that had been consecrated in church on Palm Sunday – all in order to make the cattle thrive.

> On the morning of St George's Day the animals were driven out to the fallow, the horses as well. Then George [presumably a statue of the saint] was brought out [of] the chapel and carried around the chapel. The people who were there, herdchildren as well, passed from under the image. After that George was carried around the animals.

Although this kind of eyewitness evidence for devotion to St George in the modern period is not widespread, the perceived absence probably relates more to the kinds of enquiries that researchers have undertaken rather than a lack of a lively cult; my own visit to Tbilisi in November 2012 enabled me to witness some cockerels being carried, and a rather reluctant sheep being dragged, around a church of St George in order to obtain blessings. That said, the changes in patterns of organized religion which have been experienced in parts of western Europe will have had a significant impact on this kind of patronage: Protestant traditions in general have shunned public displays where saints may appear to be presented as worthy of worship (which it is claimed should be reserved for God alone), and Roman Catholic traditions, as a result of the Counter-Reformation, also have a tendency to be wary of encouraging popular devotion to saints, especially those of questionable historicity. But the evidence is there for these areas in earlier periods if we know where to look.

Thus in medieval Finland an entire range of saints was associated with cattle, especially St Catherine of Alexandria and St Bridget of Sweden, but also St Anthony of Egypt, St Laurence, St Blaise and St Gertrude. And St George; in fact, my correspondent Katja Fält tells me that he was one of the most popular patrons of cattle in medieval Finland.[6] Meanwhile, in Italy St George is often considered to be the patron of dairies, which are, of course, concerned with the processing of some of the products of cattle and other domestic animals. It is possible that the connection is based on a belief about the predilection of dragons for sucking milk directly from cows' udders and hence affecting their yield (a similar 'crime' has sometimes been attributed to hedgehogs, to the extent that in 1566 the English parliament passed a law offering a bounty of threepence for each dead hedgehog); as a renowned dragon-slayer, St George would protect the milk, and presumably the cows too, from these unwanted attentions.

Other important evidence that identifies St George with the springtime is found in the Roma community. Roma culture is profoundly influenced by the Orthodox Christian traditions, which are strongly identified with Eastern and central Europe, as opposed to the Roman Catholic and Protestant traditions, which are rooted in western Europe. Roma people are the largest ethnic minority in the Balkans, a geographical area that encompasses nations such as Albania, Bosnia-Herzegovina, Kosovo, Montenegro, Romania and Serbia, and in common with the Eastern Orthodox Christian traditions they celebrate St George's Day on 6 May. It may be significant that Roma peoples came to Europe around 1,000 years ago from India, and hence could have brought an interest in one of the saint's Muslim or Hindu analogues with them. It is notable that the Roma call St George's Day *Ederlezi*, a name that derives from two ancient Turkish prophets Hizir and Ilyas (who seem to be forms of Al-Khidr and Elijah respectively and hence are both strongly identified as analogues of St George); 6 May has come to signify a rebirth of nature for this community just as it does for many Orthodox Christians.

In common with many faith traditions within Christianity (though not, usually, Protestantism), the celebrations start on the eve of the feast day. A first-hand account of the *Ederlezi* in 2003, in Kyustendil, south-west Bulgaria, by the journalist and author Garth Cartwright,[7] talks about a very public celebration in the communal square at the heart of the *mahala*, the poorer neighbourhood where the Roma mainly live. Cartwright notes that the Roma in Bulgaria consider St George as their own patron saint, even though St Sara is often identified in this role, especially among Roman Catholic Catalan Roma, and he reports that he asked a Bulgarian Rom singer why St George is their patron; in reply he was told something along the lines of 'when the Tzar sent a dragon to eat the Gypsies, St George saved us' – a lovely example of a localized version of the dragon-slaying legend. Music is evidently deeply significant in the festival which attracts Roma from through-out Europe. The Kyustendil celebrations included a concert on a stage by a popular musician who hailed from the local area, and later in the evening small bands of musicians (and the occasional brass band) were wandering the streets:

> As night fell bonfires began and people would dance around them as the musicians played. In the Balkans the most popu-lar form of dance is called the *hora*, a circular dance where the dancers link arms with the people on either side and skip in circles. I kept witnessing big circles of people spinning around, all very happy indeed.

The celebrations continued through the night, and as dawn broke the *mahala*'s young women headed towards the river where tradition has it that they bathe in the waters to signify rebirth. Cartwright reports that in 2003 Kyustendil's river was little more than a stream, with industry and housing needs having diverted much of its flow; bathing is no longer possible. Instead, the women cut branches from the weeping willow trees found by the watercourse.

A similar tradition relating to greenery is recorded in the Bucovina region of Romania, where people in rural areas often cut out small squares of turf, especially by the entrances to buildings, and stick willow branches into the exposed earth beneath. This custom marks St George's Day and is understood to symbolize the coming of spring. In Serbia, the celebration of the saint's feast day is linked to the ending of Turkish rule; rather like the tradition of the English Robin Hood, living as an outlaw in Sherwood Forest, Serbs recall a time when plots and plans were made in woodland hideouts. In the modern era Serbs celebrate St George's Day by preparing a container of roses and green foliage, with an egg placed in the centre. Fresh water is poured over the flowers, and if the weather is kind enough the container is placed in the garden. Children will be encouraged to wash their faces in this water and wishes for their good health are made by parents and grandparents.

On the specific point of washing on St George's Day, we have already seen that horses have been encouraged to swim – which is, in effect, the same as taking a bath. When it comes to humans, Mall Hiiemäe has recorded a number of similar practices in Estonia, such as cleaning the face with snow (recording more than twenty reports of this practice in south Estonia) or with birch sap (around a dozen reports), taking a sanitary bath (more than 80 reports, but fewer from western Estonia). These ritualized cleansings are all to be carried out on or before St George's Day, and they promise to promote a fair and unfreckled complexion and to prevent skin disease. This latter aspect links very neatly with one of St George's many special responsibilities – he is the patron saint of people suffering from scaly skin conditions, and also sometimes leprosy, probably because he overcame a 'scaly' dragon. Further evidence for the power of the saint in relation to healthy skin is found in Estonia where, as noted above, walking barefoot before St George's Day has been credited with causing skin diseases and cracked skin. This belief seems to link into a more general understanding of the earth being poisonous until vegetation has started to grow, as nature awakens at the end of winter. For example, in southeast Estonia there is a belief which says: 'Before St George's Day one must not sit on the ground as the earth has not been able to breathe yet and so it may cause diseases.'

The understanding of the earth as dangerous before St George's Day fits well with the identification of the saint as a hero who can tame the chaos and wilderness which is often associated with the dragon he defeats; the prevalence of chapels dedicated to St George at the gates of medieval city walls – for example, at Coventry in England – is one manifestation of this kind of identification, for the saint protects the town by subduing the uncivilized world beyond. It has been suggested that the dragon-slaying story can be viewed as a manifestation of very ancient beliefs playing on this identification of the dragon as a form of the dangerous natural world. In this reading the rescued princess is a form of the 'Great Mother', the positive spirit of nature who gives life to every living thing, and the dragon represents a negative, wintry power which seeks to eradicate life; St George is the hero-deity who ensures the victory of the Great Mother and thus permits the return of the spring. A standard element in the dragon legend is that the princess binds the dragon with her girdle: she uses it like a collar and lead on a dog. The girdle is a motif which is associated with some pre-Christian goddess figures, such as the Syrian Atargatis whose worship spread to Greece, Rome and beyond. Atargatis is identified as a form of the Great Mother and a fertility goddess of the earth and water, and was thought to wear a girdle that Lucian (the second-century CE rhetorician and satirist, who was ethnically Assyrian although he wrote in Greek) identified with the *cestus* of Aphrodite – a magical belt that made her irresistible.

Although there is a long tradition of noting the correspondences between St George and various pagan gods and heroes, such as the Egyptian Horus and the Roman Mithras, there has been very little work carried out on the figure of the rescued princess, and it is very difficult to know the extent to which our forebears identified this figure, and the dragon-slaying legend more generally, with the natural world and fertility rites. The placement of St George's feast day in the liturgical calendar was undoubtedly finalized well before the dragon story came to be generally connected with the saint in the twelfth century, and it is by no means unthinkable that one of the reasons why the dragon story became so popular was because it permitted the Christianization of an ancient motif of the hero-monster paradigm (and perhaps also the Great Mother) by linking it to the veneration of a figure who is himself a Christianized fertility god. We should also note the fact that during the medieval period dragon figures were paraded through the fields at Rogationtide, the Christian festival marked by processions, prayers and the physical blessing of growing crops: these large puppet dragons, manipulated as they were by humans, can be read as a controlled and defeated spirit of wintry sterility. They were not necessarily associated with St George, but it is possible that his dragon, especially when paraded in events such as the Ridings of St George, would have had some of the same meanings for the people who venerated him.

Another possible link between the dragon-slaying legend and pre-existing rituals for the celebration of spring is the significant role of the lamb, or sheep, who accompanies the princess as she goes out to meet her fate. Whilst the presence of the animal is by no means consistent in either visual or literary treatments of the narrative, it is a commonly occurring trope: a Danish tradition indicates that eggs were sacrificed to the dragon, and when the supply of eggs began to run low young people were substituted; the very oddity of this account indicates the extent to which the sheep/lamb sacrifice seems 'normal'. There are a number of examples of the inclusion of sheep in celebrations of St George's Day, especially in places which fall within the Orthodox tradition of Christianity. For example in Bulgaria, where St George's Day is known as *Gergiovden*, St George is given the title *Pobedonosez*, which means 'the Victorious', and he is particularly celebrated by shepherds. Especially in rural areas, a lamb is ceremonially killed in a ritual, known as *kurban* or *kourbania*, as an offering to St George. The lamb's horns are decorated with flowers and a prayer is read, and gates and doors are covered with flowers. It is also traditional for Bulgarian people to wash themselves in their local river (we have already noted the widespread significance of cleansing the skin on or before St George's Day), and also to weigh themselves – it seems that traditionally this was the only day of the year when Bulgarians checked their weight. Meanwhile, at Asi Gonia, Apokoronou, Crete, there is a tradition of priests blessing sheep on St George's Day; in return, the shepherds distribute free sheep's milk to local people.

We have previously noted that St George is sometimes claimed as a form of the 'Green Man', the figure found commonly in medieval

Green Man at wassailing, Fairfield Community Orchard, Lancaster.

churches as well as in contemporary 'folk' culture: everything from wall plaques to earrings featuring versions of the Green Man can be found available for sale. This motif, which is sometimes known (perhaps significantly) as the 'Green George', is often understood as a figure of fertility and the natural world although this identification is made on the basis of little hard evidence. However, we do know that in the Carinthian and Transylvanian areas of Romania farmers celebrate St George's Day by choosing a birch or willow tree which is named as the 'Green George', decking it with flowers and setting it up in the centre of their village for the feast. The following day the Green George is represented by a boy covered in branches, leaves and flowers; in the evening the Green George is a leaf-clad puppet thrown into a running stream. Versions of the Green George festival are found in Greece and some Balkan states, and although the ritual is claimed to be Christian it seems reasonable to suggest that it is a continuation of a pre-Christian tradition which can loosely be described as 'pagan'. There is often a sequence of ritual gestures that symbolize planting, harvesting and fertility, which tend to culminate with the Green George figure being thrown into water. The Green George festival and the feast of St George are celebrated on the same day, with the two figures effectively merging into one: again, we see a strong connection between St George, springtime and the celebration of new life.

Returning to our starting point of St George in the mumming plays, the motif of the combat between St George and his various human foes in these folk dramas can in itself be understood as a form of a pre-Christian tradition that understood the cycle of the year as a battle between summer and winter, personified as two warring brothers. One aspect of this story includes the idea that the defeated party journeys to the underworld, or 'Other-world'. It has been claimed that the reference to St George in the Cornish tradition recounted in the Padstow May song is a version of this story:

> O where is St George, where is he O?
> He's out in his longboat,
> All on the salt sea O!

These words occur in the dirge of songs performed as part of the 'Obby 'Oss (hobby horse) festival, which is held on 1 May and is often linked to Beltane – a pre-Christian festival marking the coming of summer rather than spring. This explanation of the song identifies the sea as a form of the 'Other-world', with St George preparing to return to land and usher in the Maying. However, this reading may be undercut by a variant reading which asks the whereabouts of 'King George', rather than 'St George', and also by the next lines in the song:

Up flies the kite and down tails the lark O,
Aunt Ursula Birdwood she had an old ewe,
And she died in her own park O!

Despite the reference to sheep here (with 'ewe' pronounced as 'yow',
a dialect form which maintains the rhyme), it is difficult to state
with any confidence that these lines relate to the legend of St George.
It seems about as likely as the contention – which is based on a
report from Brazil – that St George returned to English shores after
making a visit to South America with his wife Joan of Arc; in contrast to the pseudo-historical St George, St Joan of Arc was a real person, the heroic leader of the French army against the English,
executed as a heretic in 1431 and never married to anyone. The oral
tradition is indeed a many-splendored thing, and we need to be very
wary of the idea that modern versions of 'folk' plays are linked by an
unbroken chain to some kind of 'authentic' past.

That said, there is perhaps a suggestion that the combats between
St George and his human enemies, as found in the mummers'
plays and in some medieval imagery and narrative, do relate to the
'two brothers' motif, where a representation of summer fights with a
representation of winter. The fact that these battles between human
foes feature deaths and resurrections does tend to incline the open-
minded reader towards interpretations that identify various aspects
of St George's cult as Christianized forms of pagan rituals associated
with the return of the spring, although the evidence is clearly circum-
stantial rather than concrete. Nevertheless, the simple fact that St
George is linked so frequently to springtime (and by extension the
return of summer), and by ritualized activity in so many places in
Europe, tells its own tale.

4

St George as a Saint of Water and Healing

A fragmentary seventeenth-century manuscript in the British Library, known as Dugdale's *Book of Monuments*, contains one of our most important pieces of evidence about late medieval concepts of St George in England. Unfortunately, the information it offers is not easy to interpret, and although the manuscript has attracted much scholarly attention, in general the imagery of St George recorded in its pages has been passed over without comment. Nevertheless, the material forms a key element in our evolving understanding of how this figure came to be recognized as the patron saint of England, and the range of roles he has played in the consciousness of people who have been devoted to him.

The *Book of Monuments* was created as the result of a journey made in 1640–41, just before the outbreak of the English Civil War, at the behest of Sir Christopher Hatton, the patron of the antiquarian William Dugdale (1605–1686). The main purpose of the journey was to record a range of funerary monuments, stained glass and painted glass windows, and especially heraldry and inscriptions in English churches; Dugdale was accompanied on his travels by the artist William Sedgwick, who was employed by Hatton as an arms painter. The partial record which has survived indicates that Dugdale and Sedgwick were mainly interested in tombs and other artworks which had a direct link to the Hatton family and were thought to be at risk from iconoclasts, but they recorded various other items as they travelled around churches and cathedrals. This included the cycle of stained glass windows in the chancel windows at St George's

Church in Stamford, Lincolnshire, which dated from 1450. These windows were indeed destroyed during the Civil War so the fact of Dugdale's and Sedgwick's visit, and their decision to record what they saw, is fortuitous indeed, albeit that the record which survives is clearly incomplete.

Before the destruction, the windows probably included 29 separate images taken from the life of St George, each arranged over a more-or-less fanciful portrait of a Founder Knight of the Order of the Garter. The man who commissioned and paid for the windows was William Bruges (*c.* 1375–1450); he was the most eminent herald in England, and bore the title Garter King of Arms. This post was created in 1415 and Bruges was the first man to hold it, although the Order of the Garter had been in existence for more than 60 years by that point. As far as we can tell, Bruges was travelling through Lincolnshire when he came across a ruinous church dedicated to St George in the town of Stamford. Because this saint was the patron of the Order of the Garter, the royal chivalric order with which Bruges was intimately concerned, he decided to spend a considerable amount of money on rebuilding parts of the church and generally putting it to rights; in time he was buried there. His generous donation included commissioning a full glazing scheme in the rebuilt chancel, the part of the church that houses the altar.

It is likely that Bruges did not live long enough to see the completion of his plans, but it is at least possible that he was concerned with the choice of imagery which graced the chancel windows in a two-tier format. The sequence of portraits of the Founder Knights of the Order of the Garter in the lower range was an obvious choice for a man in his position – although the fact that he may not have had secure knowledge about which men were counted in the first group of Garter Knights has allowed a number of military and royal historians to spend many happy hours arguing over who exactly is depicted and whether or not they actually were involved in the Order from the outset. By contrast, the narrative of St George which occupied the register above the Founder Knights has attracted relatively little attention, although it is required viewing for anyone who is serious about the study of St George's cult.

One of the major problems with the record of the Stamford glass in Dugdale's *Book of Monuments* is that it is clearly unfinished. A number of the images have not been fully coloured in – which in some cases is a blessing, especially where the more graphic images of torture are missing the full effect of the bloody assault – but the more pressing omission is that the entire first window, which would have contained four lights and hence eight images (four from the life of St George and four of the Founder Knights), is entirely unrecorded. This is very clear from the fact that the inscription on the relevant page announces the first image to be a record of the second window. It may be that the first window had already been so damaged by the time Dugdale and Sedgwick arrived that it was not thought worthy of being recorded; an alternative explanation is that the notes or sketches of the first window were misplaced before a fair copy could be produced. It is generally felt that the version of the manuscript in the British Library was not created on site but was intended as a presentation copy for the patron, Sir Christopher Hatton – the work is demonstrably incomplete, but this need not necessarily imply that another, lost version, had the whole work recorded. Whatever the truth of the matter, we have only 21 images where there probably ought to be 29, and the beginning of the narrative is part of what is missing.

Furthermore, the sequence as we have it starts with a puzzle. The opening image from the narrative of St George as Sedgwick recorded it is shown opposite. It is unlike any other visualization of the saint that I know. A man brandishing a sword stands before a well, and a woman and a jug lie on the ground; water flows from the latter. The man has a halo, or nimbus, but no other identifying attribute – there is no sign of the armour and red cross that St George wears in subsequent images from the cycle, but it seems very likely that this figure is meant to be read as St George. We cannot know, though, what he is meant to be doing. Has he forced the woman to the ground, or is he about to rescue her from some unseen villain? Is the jug actually a misinterpretation of something else, such as a swaddled infant?

The literary scholar Jennifer Fellows has drawn my attention to *Le Roman d'Auberon*, an early fourteenth-century French text which

William Sedgwick, 'St George at the Well', showing stained glass windows in St George's Church, Stamford, Lincolnshire (*c.* 1450). From William Dugdale, *Book of Monuments* (*c.* 1641).

contains a complex and apparently unparalleled narrative of our hero. The Auberon of the title is the twin brother of St George – their parents, delightfully enough, are said to be Julius Caesar and Morgan le Fay (half-sister of King Arthur, who is claimed by the French as much as the English and Welsh). In the relevant section of the story St George is described as the lover of the Sultan of Egypt's daughter, at the time when the Holy Family were escaping from Herod's evil plan to kill baby boys and hence prevent fulfilment of the prophecy that a child born in Bethlehem would depose him and become king of the Jews; there is no concern about the anachronism of an early fourth-century saint meeting Christ three centuries earlier. The princess reveals that she is pregnant, and she flees from her father with St George. Stopping to rest by a fountain on Mount Noiron, the saint has a battle with a serpent – he manages to kill it, but the sight of his wounds induces an early labour in his paramour. She insists that he leaves her alone, but the Virgin Mary, St Joseph and the Christ Child then appear, just in time to help with the delivery of the new baby, who, it is claimed, will grow up to become the apostle and evangelist St Mark. The Virgin then washes her own son in the water of the fountain, and bids St George bathe in it next. Healed and refreshed by the water, he then rides off in search of food, meeting 34 brigands as he goes. He kills three, but some of the others contrive to find the Holy Family and the princess, and steal the newborn baby as well as St Joseph's moustaches and staff. Luckily St George meets them again, kills them and retrieves the stolen baby and St Joseph's property (whereupon the Virgin Mary miraculously restores the severed moustaches).

The mysterious image from Stamford could be a reference to this story, especially if the fallen jug is actually a misreading of a swaddled baby; perhaps the woman on the ground is a mistake for the recumbent princess, resting after having given birth. The slip could be explained by the likelihood that neither Sedgwick nor Dugdale were familiar with this medieval French story – they may have thought of St George as a saint who married his rescued princess and brought her home to Coventry, as claimed in Richard Johnson's *Seven Champions of Christendom* (1576–80), and failed to recognize this vision of him as a knight who impregnated his Egyptian lover and accidentally caused her to give birth by a remote fountain. If the fifteenth-century artist who designed the glass was not familiar with the story either, or if the craftspeople who created the image lacked this knowledge, then it is easy to see how the subject may have moved away from what was originally intended: the fountain becomes a well, the labouring mother becomes a woman lying on the ground, the baby becomes a jug. Furthermore, the window may have been damaged and this scene at the well could have been Sedgwick's best guess of what it was meant to show; he may have been reliant on local knowledge which itself was based on unreliable recollections. On balance it seems unlikely that the image is meant to show the French legend, not least because of the problematic absence of the Virgin Mary from the subject. She plays a key role in the story as the midwife of the princess and the progenitor of St George's healing – and she is very evident in several of the subsequent images, which relate to the narrative of St George being resurrected and made Our Lady's Knight.

Whether or not the fallen jug was actually meant to be a swaddled baby, we can be sure that the scene is taking place by a well. This means that the work is one of a small handful of clear linkages between St George and water in Britain. The name of St George's Channel, which lies between the coasts of southwest Wales and southeast Ireland, is another example, and, as we have previously noted, there is a healing well reputed to cure or protect from equine diseases in the Welsh hamlet of St George, also known as Llan Sain Siôr (historically Denbighshire, now Conwy). There is also an invocation of the saint travelling by boat in the traditional Padstow May song, from Cornwall, also noted in the previous chapter. However, when we look abroad we find many more examples of a connection between the saint and water. It is notable that his analogues in both Islam and Hinduism are especially associated with a well of immortal life, and it is likely that the modern English absence of connection is the exception rather than the rule.

Thus we find that in Lebanon laypeople claim that St George rides across the sea on his horse on his feast day; in time of drought the saint will strike the surface of the sea with his sword to make water rise to the sky, so it may then fall as rain. St George is recognized here as the patron saint of sailors, and the protector of navigation and ships in general, as well as functioning as the herald of springtime.[1] The commentator Marlène Kanaan has claimed that Lebanese sailors call upon the saint for help when a storm is brewing and before putting to sea,[2] and further notes that the Ottoman navy had the same habits – again underlining the idea that interest in St George/Mar Jiryis/Al-Khidr is both widespread and profoundly significant in much of the eastern Mediterranean despite differences in religion, ethnicity and culture.

The previous chapter discussed the significance of St George as a harbinger of spring, and much of the evidence linking the saint, and his analogues, to water can be seen as an aspect of this broad tradition. Thus we note that at the culmination of the ritual of the Green George in a number of countries in Eastern Europe the figure is cast into running water – this may be a relic of water worship as much as a celebration of a personification of the fertility of the earth. Placing a bowl of fresh water outside the house plays a significant role in the springtime festivities in Serbia, and there are many records of bathing on St George's Day (both humans and horses) to promote good health. These kinds of ideas have largely disappeared from the historical record in Britain, but I feel that the likelihood is just that – they have disappeared, rather than never having existed in the first place.

By contrast, wells of St George are certainly known abroad, such as the two *fontaines de St Georges* in Normandy; one location, Fontaine-le-Bourg (Seine-Maritime), had a localized legend of St George in addition to a healing well dedicated to him. Several local sayings invoking St George also survive in Normandy: they primarily relate to agriculture, and hence utilize a memorable feast day which falls in the spring in order to record advice about planting days through an oral tradition. This fits well with the evidence discussed in the previous chapter, but we should note that the importance of St George in Normandy is quite remarkable, going well beyond a feast day which falls conveniently for agricultural purposes. It is sometimes thought that it might be a legacy of the English occupation of this area in the early fifteenth century. However, there is clear evidence that the cult was well established far in advance of the English arrival; indeed, Normandy was the area where St George's cult seems really to have taken root in France. In late medieval Normandy there were nearly 70 parish churches dedicated to St George, with four sites holding relics of the saint, seven settlements where an annual fair of St George was held, three towns with confraternities (or 'associations') of St George and a further community where an annual feast of St George was held. One town, Colomby (Manche), even had a special song of St George which was sung on his feast day.

The saint was known and venerated in Gaul from at least the sixth century, and in the middle of the eighth century an apparently miraculous event took place that seems to have led to a marked upsurge in the cult. A contemporary chronicler relates that during the time of Abbot Austrulph (743–53) a coffer was washed up on a beach near Portbail in the Cotentin region of Normandy, and was retrieved by local people. When opened by the religious and civic authorities, the coffer proved to hold a beautiful parchment book of the Gospels in Latin, and a reliquary which contained part of the jaw-bone of St George, relics of various other saints and a piece of the True Cross, as well as letters to authenticate all the treasures. Suitably impressed, Count Richwin, the governor of Cotentin, and the religious leaders decided to allow God to choose where these gifts should be taken. They placed the coffer and its contents in an ox cart, let the animals wander at will, and followed as the cart was pulled inland to the hilltop settlement of Brix. It was decided to build a church to the honour of St George there, and at Richwin's insistence two fur-ther sanctuaries were built, one in honour of the Virgin and one to St Cross; many miracles were witnessed at the new church complex. One (French) commentator has claimed that the coffer was being sent by Pope Zacharias as a gift to the English Church when 'the hand of God' redirected it to the Normans, who were presumably thought to be more deserving!

A key point in this anecdote is that the relics were travelling by sea. It could be that they washed up on the beach as the result of a shipwreck, and if Pope Zacharias was indeed sending the relics to England he presumably would have put them on a boat. However, medieval saints' legends sometimes contain references to objects that move around on or in water without the need for any kind of vessel – altar stones come to mind – and it is by no means impossible that the coffer was thought to have travelled of its own accord, or as a result of specific divine guidance. Certainly the latter is more plausible when we consider evidence for St George as a patron of mariners – it would be a very bad omen for his abilities in this regard if a ship containing his relics was to founder. We will shortly discuss a story of St George in one of his eastern Mediterranean guises – Mar Jiryis

– appearing in the sea to prevent a boat removing a healing stone from a church dedicated to him, and this type of incident may lead us to conclude that he has some kind of link to a pre-Christian water deity, or that he represents an effort to Christianize pre-existing water-worship cults, but it is very difficult to demonstrate these sorts of influences with any certainty. Some authors are keen to link St George to 'pagan' traditions which they claim are the 'true' British belief system, based, for example, on the reference to St George in his longboat in the song from Padstow, but I am reluctant to read too much into what may simply be a group of parallels and coincidences. My own view is that St George has acted as a patron of all sorts of concepts, including horses, skin disease, dairying and, on occasion, seafaring, and his link to water, while significant, should not be claimed to be *particularly* significant in an English context.

That said, there may well have been more evidence of this kind a few centuries ago, just as many of the links between the saint and the natural world are largely obscured in modern England. One of the reasons underlying my sense of a 'lost' tradition of St George and water in British, and especially English, experience, is that we find so many examples of linkages between the two concepts elsewhere, both within and outside Christian traditions. We have already enumerated some European, and hence Christian, examples, but St George's analogues in Islam and Hinduism both have a strong connection to water too. Al-Khidr – the Green One – is said to have turned entirely green in consequence of bathing three times in the Fountain of Immortality; the fact that he leaves green footprints wherever he goes may imply that he has never quite dried out after his final dip.

An important tradition of Al-Khidr involves a stream and a ship. This story derives from an understanding that Moses (known as Musa in Islamic tradition) and his servant went in search of a wise teacher;[3] a vision told them that they would have found the right place when fish they were carrying escaped and swam away; the moment was missed when Musa was asleep, but once it was dinner time the servant confessed to the loss of the fish and they hurriedly retraced their steps. A partly hooded man was waiting for them at the propitious spot, and by his bearing Musa recognized Al-Khidr as the teacher he sought. Al-Khidr agreed to teach Musa, but warned that great patience was needed to learn from him. Al-Khidr was not to be questioned about any of his actions.

First the three travellers embarked on a ship, which Al-Khidr proceeded to scuttle. Musa was appalled and asked Al-Khidr whether he was trying to drown people. Al-Khidr replied that he would need patience, as he had been warned. Next they met a boy, whom Al-Khidr killed. Musa again questioned the sage, but was reminded that he would need patience. Finally they came to a town where they asked for food but were denied. In the town was a wall on the point of collapse, and Al-Khidr set it to rights. Musa could not help himself and expressed his bemusement.

Al-Khidr said that this was the final straw and the two men must now part ways, but first he would interpret these strange actions which Musa had been unable to be patient about. The ship belonged to poor people working the sea, but a king was seeking to take possession of the craft by force; Al-Khidr made a fault in it that would render it of no further interest to this avaricious monarch, but which could be repaired easily when the danger had passed. The boy was intending to rebel against his god-fearing parents, and they would be given a better son in exchange for him. The wall belonged to two orphans, the sons of a righteous man; under it was a great treasure. The boys would find it once they reached adulthood, and repairing the wall would keep it safe from the unworthy people they lived among. This story fits in with the understanding of Al-Khidr as a wanderer and a practitioner of mystic arts. As we have seen, Al-Khidr (even when known by his alternative appellations) is reputed to have found the Fountain of Immortality, or of Youth, or the Well of Life, which is said to be located near the confluence of the Mediterranean and the Red Sea: this is likely to be where the fish escaped in this story.

One final point worth noting in relation to watery associations is that St George's role as a dragon-slayer may be a somewhat veiled reference to this theme. Our modern reading of dragon imagery and dragon legends tends to stress the allegories of heresy and evil which we see encoded in these monsters, but we must not overlook the simple fact that many of our forebears believed that dragons were literal creatures of flesh and blood with real powers to spread pestilence, to threaten life and limb, and – significantly – to contaminate water supplies. In 1725 Henry Bourne, a Newcastle curate, wrote that the custom of lighting bonfires on Midsummer Eve was derived from the desire to frighten dragons away: the monsters 'being incited to lust through the heat of the season, did frequently, as they flew through the Air, Spermatize in the Wells and Fountains'.[4] This kind of perceived connection between dragons and water, and especially the pollution of water, may imply that St George's role as a dragon-slayer allowed him to protect watercourses.

An intriguing piece of evidence that links St George to wells in a rather different way derives from Palestine, where the saint is commonly credited with rescuing people who happen to fall down wells or into deep pits. My correspondent Dan Koski tells me that his wife's grandfather claimed that just this experience happened to him when he was a young man;[5] I asked him whether the intercession took the form of a personal rescue by a manifestation of the saint himself or a less direct intervention, such as a prayer to the saint having been closely followed by the arrival of human rescuers. Koski told me that until his dying day the grandfather insisted that St George had manifested in physical form and bodily lifted him out of the well. Koski suggests that the link between St George and well rescues may be derived from the narrative tradition that he was thrown into a pit and kept there for three days during the period of his torture: if he is right then the fact of wells containing water is a side issue. We should also be aware that St George is not usually associated with saving people from drowning (St Nicholas is the more common patron in this circumstance). Koski also notes that there is not much evidence of healing wells of St George in his part of Palestine, and makes the useful observation that there may be a general sense not to overtax the saint with too many requests.

Back in Britain, besides the healing well for horses in the Welsh hamlet of St George, there is also a St George's well at Padstow – the name extends to be used as the name of a beach there, and a St George's Cove is nearby. St George's name is invoked by a number of craft brewers as they label their products and there is even a St George's Brewery at Malvern in Worcestershire, and a St George's Distillery in Norfolk. As the first operational whisky distillery in England for more than 100 years it is named simply in honour of the national patron, and the connection with the derivation of the term whisky – the Scottish Gaelic *uisge beatha* translates as 'water of life' – is probably no more than a particularly happy coincidence. Nevertheless, it can be argued that a connection between St George and water is creeping back into popular consciousness.

St George as a Healer

While looking for the scarce links between St George and water in England, I was delighted to come across an eighteenth-century record of a spa (given as 'spaw' in the original) on St George's Fields in Southwark, London, in a newspaper advertisement published in 1773:

> St. George's Spaw, Dog and Duck, St. George's Fields. The Waters of this Spaw are now in their utmost perfection, and to be had at 6d. per gallon . . . These waters are recommended by the most eminent physicians, for the cure of the rheumatism, stone, gravel, fistulas, ulcers, cancers, sore eyes, and in all kinds of scorbutic cases whatever; and are remarkable for restoring a lost appetite . . . A cold bath from the above mineral. The long room fitted up for large entertainments. Tea, coffee and hot rolls as usual.[6]

This advertisement neatly links St George and water with the concept of him as a healer, and, of course, as a useful commercial motif. We know that a three-year lease of the main part of the Bridge House holdings, including the 'mineral spring' at the Dog and Duck, was leased to Mrs Elizabeth Hedger at this time for about £50 a year: she clearly intended to capitalize on her investment.

St George's Fields in Southwark has quite a notable history. It had been a significant location of political disorder only five years before Mrs Hedger was advertising the benefits of her spa, as a result of the journalist, radical, reformer, outlaw and parliamentarian John Wilkes returning to England from exile in France in 1768 (mainly to escape his creditors, it seems). He stood as an anti-government candidate for Middlesex in the parliamentary elections and was duly victorious but, once elected, Wilkes was arrested in relation to an obscenity charge, and taken to King's Bench Prison in Southwark. For the next fortnight a large crowd assembled at St George's Fields, which formed a convenient expansive open space by the prison. On 10 May 1768 around 15,000 people were outside the prison. The crowd chanted 'Wilkes and Liberty!', 'No Liberty, No King!' and 'Damn the King! Damn the Government! Damn the Justices!' Fearing that the crowd would attempt to rescue Wilkes, the troops opened fire, killing seven people in an event sometimes known as the St George's Fields Massacre. Anger at the behaviour of the military led to a spate of disturbances all over London, including a riot at a theatre in Drury Lane which was staging a play written by one of Wilkes's opponents. Wilkes himself was expelled from parliament and then was re-elected and expelled several times more, but found time to become a strong proponent of the principle of press freedom, helping to enshrine it in British law.

St George's Fields provides an interesting link between St George and radical politics of the eighteenth century, a link that probably owes more to the location of the King's Bench Prison than to a specific connection between this saint and political consciousness. That said, we should also note that St George's Hill at Weybridge in Surrey was occupied by the agrarian-socialist (or even proto-communist) sect known as the True Levellers, or the Diggers, for five months in the summer of 1649, during the period of political turmoil following the execution of Charles I; the same site was occupied by a group called The Land is Ours in 1995 and 1999, so there does seem to be some possibility of correlation between locations named for this saint and political activism.

For our current purposes the most significant aspect of St George's Fields is the fact that it was for many years the home of the Bethlem Royal Hospital, one of the world's oldest hospitals for the treatment of mental illness and the original of the term

'Bedlam'. The hospital was founded in 1247 as the Priory of St Mary of Bethlehem on a site now covered by Liverpool Street station. By the fourteenth century it was already treating the insane; in 1547 it came under the control of the City of London as one of five 'Royal' hospitals re-founded after the Reformation; the hospital moved to Moorfields in 1675, and then to its third site in 1815, due to increased numbers of patients and a crumbling premises. This new building was at St George's Fields, Southwark, part of which still survives as the Imperial War Museum.

The fact of the Bethlem Royal Hospital relocating to St George's Fields is almost certainly a coincidence with, rather than a reflection of, the saint's strong connection with healing in general and psychiatric illness in particular. Other philanthropic organizations, such as the Magdalen Hospital for Penitent Prostitutes and the Philanthropic Society, also relocated to St George's Fields, apparently in order to take advantage of clean air and water and to escape the squalor and overcrowding of the City of London. Nevertheless, it is not difficult to find healthcare institutions that invoke St George's patronage – most obviously, there is St George's Hospital in Tooting, London, which was founded in 1773 at Hyde Park Corner. This hospital moved to its current site, which it shares with St George's Hospital Medical School, in 1976. This important education and research facility was established in 1733, also at Hyde Park Corner, and was one of the first institutions in England to provide formal training courses for doctors.

Moving further afield, there is a great deal of evidence for historic and contemporary devotion to St George which relates to health issues in Palestine. One undated account is set in a Christian church dedicated to him under the name Mar Jiryis. A priest was administering Communion in the 'Greek fashion', where the consecrated bread is crumbled into the chalice and the mixture is spooned into the mouth of communicants. The priest contrived to spill some of this holy substance onto his foot, where it burned a hole right through to the floor and left a mark on the flagstone below. The unfortunate priest died of his wound, but a diseased man later knelt on the stained flagstone, quite unaware of its significance, and was miraculously healed. Many other healings subsequently took place on this stone, until the Sultan of the Muscovites decided that he must have the stone for himself. The local religious leader, a friend of the Sultan, agreed, and the stone was extracted from the floor and taken overland to Joppa without incident. However, once it had been loaded onto a boat Mar Jiryis himself appeared in the sea and pushed the boat with his lance back to the shore. The Sultan then realized his mistake, and arranged for the stone to be returned to its original place with all due ceremony. The message seems to be that St George/Al-Khidr/Mar Jiryis will aid those who call upon him, but his aid is not to be taken for granted and he will personally intervene if his shrines are not treated with sufficient respect.

Today the town of Beit Jala, south of Jerusalem, has a predominantly Palestinian Christian community and a substantial Muslim minority, and the saint is regularly invoked as a healer by both communities. Beit Jala is a major centre for the veneration of St George (his popularity ranks alongside that of St Nicholas, the original 'Santa Claus', who is said to have stayed in Beit Jala while on pilgrimage). Dan Koski has provided me with a number of examples of ways in which St George's intercession as a healer is invoked. For instance, parents of children who have speech problems often go to the local monastery on a Sunday and ask the priest to put a key in the child's mouth. Koski tells me that this practice is common with both Christians and Muslims, and that his own father-in-law experienced it when he was a young boy. St George is also invoked for sight problems, especially blindness. General health issues are covered too: Palestinians will use holy oil from St George – derived from his tomb at Lod – and make the sign of the cross with the oil on the part of the body that is afflicted and then on their forehead and hands. Koski also tells me that people with mental health issues would sometimes be chained up in the courtyard overnight in the hope that the saint would heal them, and this fits with evidence that the 'chains of St George', kept in a number of churches and chapels dedicated to him in places such as Cairo and Al-Khader, are used as a way of promoting healing – sufferers wrap the chains around themselves and also kiss them. Presumably each example of these chains is thought to relate to the time when St George was imprisoned, during the period when he was tortured for his Christian beliefs.

My overall feeling when reviewing the evidence linking St George with water and healing is that the English tradition of this devotion has lost some of its original form, perhaps as a result of the concentration on the motif of the saint as a dragon-slayer, and that it will probably be impossible to recover it. It could be that the mysterious Stamford image is the last remaining reference to an English story of St George as a rainmaker, or even to a legend that is related to the idea of a well which confers immortality – as we have seen, both these ideas are associated with his analogues in other religious traditions – but unless some previously overlooked or unrecognized evidence comes to light it seems unlikely that we can ever speak of this aspect of the tradition with certainty. However, it is worth bearing in mind the possibility that the popularity of St George-themed ales produced by English brewers may have more than simple patriotism behind it: the fact of the drought-ending well-rescuer, who bathed in waters of immortality and who slayed a water-dwelling and polluting dragon, being invoked through the naming of beer may be no more than coincidence, but it is a particularly appropriate one.

5
St George as a Dragon-slayer

For all his symbolic guises as martyr, healer, fertility-bringer and guardian, for many – possibly even the vast majority – of his devotees around the world, St George is above all the hero who took on a dragon in single combat. This element of the cult is certainly the most obvious to the casual observer, for it is frequently invoked in coinage, pub signs and commercial insignia, and it is also the most discussed, exercising what can feel like an endless fascination for commentators.

This ubiquity is both a blessing and a curse. On the positive side it means that virtually everyone has some kind of concept of St George, something that cannot be said with confidence of more obscure dragon-encountering saints like St Carantoc and St Martha. However, the imagery of St George's dragon-slaying exploits often feels so commonplace that it can be hard to persuade viewers to get beyond its comfortable familiarity to question what it might represent at a deeper level; it also beguiles enthusiasts into difficult culs-de-sac which shift the emphasis away from what was believed about St George, and why, by our forebears, and towards unanswerable questions. Do dragons have any claim to be recognized as 'real'? Are dragon stories based on misunderstandings of dinosaur fossils, or crocodile carcasses, or other such 'authentic' creatures? Where exactly did St George kill his dragon? A lot of energy has been spent pursuing these trails, rarely to any useful outcome. From an English perspective, it can be hard to defend a patron saint whose historical uncertainty is rounded off by a decidedly unrealistic episode involving a fire-breathing monster which appeals to the popular imagination far more than to hard-headed academics, religious commentators and nervous politicians.

It is clear that the concept of dragons, broadly defined, has existed over many centuries – the simple fact that every recorded human culture seems to have some version of the hero-fights-monster story is testament to this. In most cases this is a narrative that amounts to human-fights-monster-to-rescue-maiden: examples include the classical myths of Perseus and Andromeda, Roger and Angélique, and Hercules and Hesione. These types of stories occur in a wide range of sources, from the earliest recorded creation myth, the *Epic of Gilgamesh*, to very localized legends of named heroes fighting very particular creatures – in England the story of the Lambton Worm, a huge dragon fought by the heroic Sir John Lambton of County Durham, is a good example – which often seem to be a way of explaining a landscape feature or a heraldic device.

Dragons can be imbued with all sorts of meanings. In Europe these are often negative concepts such as chaos, disease and pollution;[1] they also act as a foil to the heroic human who takes them on and subdues them, nullifying their effect on the community that they have threatened and simultaneously bringing glory to himself (more rarely herself) and also allowing a transference of power through an osmosis-like process whereby the victor takes on the strength of the defeated enemy. Dragons can be represented in a wide range of contexts, from the profoundly religious to the scabrously secular, and carry a wealth of connotations. We can perhaps see them as a convenient imagining of the 'other' which enables tale tellers to present their (super)human hero to the best advantage, containing and/or nullifying a powerful threat.

In common with other monsters, dragons are tremendously useful as vehicles of meaning: the word 'monster' comes from the same root as 'demonstrate', an etymological link that points to the ways in which stories of monsters can be employed to teach viewers and listeners lessons about the correct way to live and the risks you run by wandering from the path of righteousness. The extent to which they have permeated human consciousness leads me to assert, with apologies to Voltaire, that if dragons did not exist it would be necessary to invent them. So the question of their verisimilitude is, for me at least, a non-question: it simply does not matter whether they had any historical reality when their usefulness and ubiquity are so clearly established.

Once we start to move away from the simple question of 'were dragons real?' to the more interesting issue of 'why have people referred to dragons so frequently in their stories and imagery?' all kinds of complexities become apparent. One strong theme in understandings of dragons is that they do not have a fixed form: they can be winged or unwinged; have two legs, four legs or none at all; have one head or several; breathe fire or spread contagion through their exhalations. They can be as small as a cat or bigger than an elephant, even before their wingspan comes into the equation. Dragons abound in sculpture, paintings, stained glass and other art forms; these visual treatments demonstrate further variations, with colours ranging from red, pink, yellow and orange to browns and greens, and an equivalent variation in ferocity. They sometimes have the ability to fly (even the kinds without wings) and often embody aspects of recognizably dangerous animals, such as wolves, bears, dogs, lions and – most obviously – snakes. This shape-shifting ability (actually an inherent *instability*) is a handy cipher of the extent to which the concept of the dragon is malleable, and can be used to embody a wide variety of meanings according to context, the narrative demands of the story and the needs of the community who are the audience for that story.

Dragons are often understood to live in wet or marshy places, especially in European tradition; the fact that St George is associated with water, as we saw in the previous chapter, may well indicate one of the reasons why the dragon fitted into his cult so easily. It can also be argued that Christianity 'needed' a dragon-slaying story in order to evangelize effectively in societies that were accustomed to this narrative form – the saga of *Beowulf* is just one example of a use of the motif in a context that is clearly intended to reflect a pre-Christian world. There are a large number of dragon-slaying saints – St Michael is the most well known of the 'also-rans' – but St George is undoubtedly the best regarded of the group. It is hard to disentangle his popularity as a dragon-slayer from his popularity more generally, and hence to establish whether his cult became so widespread because of the inclusion of this motif, or whether the motif was successfully included because the cult was so popular anyway. What is not in doubt, however, is the extent to which this element of St George has tended to overshadow the rest of his identifications, connections and patronages, especially in the modern era.

We now turn to consider four specimen images of St George and the dragon from the canon of western European art. The ones I have chosen are not particularly well known; I have resisted the temptation to include instantly recognizable images such as Vittore Carpaccio's black-armoured, helmetless hero of the Scuola di San Giorgio degli Schiavoni in Venice, upon which John Ruskin based the badge of the Guild of St George, or the version of the combat used in the symbolism of the Order of the Garter. Instead I have opted to use images which I feel can help us to draw out some of the range of different meanings that have been portrayed and explored through this motif at various times from the late medieval era to the present day.

Our first image is an English painted glass panel from around 1505, which was made as part of a scheme of glazing for the house of John Wygston, a merchant in the provincial town of Leicester. Although this was a domestic setting, the windows included religious as well as secular imagery in a way that was typical of the late Middle Ages – the sharp divide that modern people tend to perceive between the spiritual and the temporal would be unfamiliar to many medievals – and this underlines the extent to which saints, and indeed monsters, could play a role in the profane world just as much as the sacred realm.

The image shows St George as an armoured knight, with his sword in his left hand and a spear in his right. He is trampling the dragon under his feet, and his identity, and indeed his saintly status, is confirmed by the nimbus, or halo, around his head. The dragon is a fearsome beast; it is winged, toothed and clawed, and has a second head at the end of its tail. The model for this presentation seems to be the snake-like amphisbaena, a staple of the medieval bestiary, or the book of beasts – a collection of images and short descriptions of a variety of animals and birds, both real and imaginary, which often include a moralizing explanation.[2] The standard medieval bestiary text talks about the amphisbaena as a duplicitous beast who uses its two heads to tell twice as many lies – it is literally 'two faced'. In case we were in any doubt about the ill intent of the creature shown here, the second head of the monster is trying to bite into the saint's thigh, revealing its sharp teeth as it does so. This head sits at the end of a long, snake-like tail, which curls around the saint's leg in the manner of a boa constrictor – again a bestiary reference, where the dragon is described as 'the greatest of snakes', which attempts to crush its enemy, the elephant, to death in its suffocating coils. The bestiary explains that coils of the dragon's tail are like the snares of sin, and the saint's apparent disregard for the actions of the snake-like tail is perhaps a sign of the extent to which he is able to transcend such physical distractions. A similar treatment can be seen in the Rossetti image on page 31, from the nineteenth century, which suggests that this is a very long-lived motif.

The primary head of the dragon is also equipped with sharp teeth, but it has the additional motif of a pointed tongue, formed to resemble an arrow, or perhaps the point of the spear that St George is using to assail the creature through both jaws. The dragon's two feet are decked out with curved claws, some of which are trying to pierce the armour on St George's lower right leg, though they seem to be making little impact. The foremost foot is not attacking any particular part of the saint's body, but its positioning seems to be far from accidental. It lies alongside, and perhaps gestures with its claws towards, a clearly marked orifice at the base of the tail.

The presence of this orifice could imply an anus – the display of which would identify the monster as a base creature – or the site of a previous wound, albeit in an anatomically significant location.[3] However, it is more likely that it actually marks the dragon as female; this glass panel is an example of quite a large number of St George's dragons presented in this way. Through extensive research I have established that the period around the end of the fifteenth century and the start of the sixteenth century saw a vogue for presenting St George's dragon as female. This motif is occasionally found in texts

Stained glass panel of St George and the dragon, Leicester, *c.* 1505.

(such as Alexander Barclay's *Life of St George*, 1515, where the dragon is consistently referred to as 'she'), but it more commonly occurs in sculpture, painting, engraving and other visual imagery. In most examples, as in this panel, there are visible female genitalia, though occasionally breasts or dugs are also shown, and in some cases one or more baby dragonlets are depicted that seem to be intended to identify the dragon as a mother. There are also common postural motifs, such as the dragon lying on her back with her pudenda exposed, as if she is offering herself to the saint – 'don't kill me, have sex with me instead' – and there is frequently a broken lance, spear or a thigh bone pointing directly to the orifice. In this example there is no clear indicating object, other than perhaps the dragon's own foot, but another very common motif is certainly present – the spearing into the mouth. This is a very consistent visual trope in the lexicon of images of female dragons with St George, and it seems to play on the idea of the mouth as a double of the vagina. Connected ideas are the *vagina dentata*, or toothed vagina, and advice to medieval midwives to encourage a labouring mother to open her mouth. It is interesting to note that the bestiary takes quite a different approach to the monster, advising that the danger of dragons lies in their tail rather than their teeth, and this idea of the boa constrictor-like tail is also found in hero legends which occur outside of the corpus of St George narratives and imagery: this focus on the mouth is by no means a simple repetition of a standard formulation of dragons per se.

I am sometimes asked what the genitalia of dragons (if they were real animals!) would actually look like. Given that, of all the creatures dragons seem to correspond to most, they are primarily identified as reptilian, the answer is that they would not have genitalia at all – they would have a cloaca, the cavity into which the intestinal, urinary and generative canals open in birds, reptiles, amphibians, some fish and all but higher mammals. Could it be, then, that the orifice is meant to represent a cloaca? The best answer I can come up with is 'possibly', but it needs to be borne in mind that reptiles definitely do not have breasts or dugs, although dragons apparently do, and this again reminds us that we are not dealing with 'real' animals, but with malleable products of the imagination. Furthermore, St George's dragons are sometimes shown with two orifices, one behind the other in the same arrangement as the vagina and the anus, and indeed there is one example where the dragon is clearly endowed with a very human-looking scrotum (and is standing on its legs rather than lying on its back as the 'female' dragons almost invariably do), so medieval artists evidently were able to conceptualize dragons in relation to human genitalia. We should not overlook the fact that the weaponry used by St George, the sword and spear or lance, is overtly phallic: the artist may be telling us that the saint is sublimating his sexual desires through attacking the monster. As we have seen, St George is often associated with chastity, so this reading confirms the idea that he is rejecting the implicit sexual offer made by the dragon, just as he transcends the sinful snare of her tail; he is not tempted by her dangerous feminine and fleshly wiles, but attacks her instead.

In default of any detailed notes made by an artist explaining why a certain dragon looks the way it does we can only surmise about what is going on, but the evidence does seem to suggest that the presence of an orifice, especially in association with the postural clues, the presence of a pointer and other factors, is intended to be understood as marking the dragon as female. Given that virtually all the artworks created in the pre-modern period were made to order, as the result of a specific commission, it is clear that some kind of thought process about encoding the dragon as evil underlay this presentation – medieval images of dragons often incorporate aspects of fierce and potentially dangerous creatures like snakes, lions, bears and dogs, but the labelling of the dragon as female and sexual goes well beyond this simple negative construction. The presentation of the dragon-with-orifice, apparently offering herself sexually in an attempt to save her own life, labels her not simply as female, but as a degenerate, sexualized female, in contrast to the chaste, heroic and privileged masculinity of the saint.

Our second image is about half a century later in date, and visually far more complex. It is a German engraving; it dates from the Reformation period and wears its religious allegiance very clearly. We see the infant Christ, in the guise of St George, mounted on a large horse and spearing a recumbent, many-headed monster. They are located in a barren landscape outside a ruined building, with a townscape in the background featuring two twin-spired buildings. The maiden who is being rescued, along with her lamb, is almost hidden in the middle ground, to the right of the taller spires. The maiden can be interpreted as a form of the 'true' Reformed Church, which is being saved by Christ/St George from the Catholic 'heresy' – the

Peter Gottland, *St George and the Dragon: Allegory of the Triumph
of the New Faith over the Old*, 1552, engraving.

latter is embodied in the dragon. This identification is crystallized by
the fact that one of the monstrous heads wears an ornate triple-
tiered headdress in reference to the papal tiara; the creature is thus
an embodiment of both the Catholic Church in general and the
pope (always a target for Reformers' attacks) in particular. A figure
of God the Father looks down from heaven and sends forth the
Holy Spirit, in the conventional form of a dove: this is very reminiscent of many medieval images of the Annunciation, where the
Archangel Gabriel tells the Virgin Mary that she will conceive Christ.
In these images God the Father is often visible in the sky, sending
either the dove or a small figure of Christ towards the Virgin, sometimes down a sunbeam. The artist's intention here seems to be to
indicate that God approves of what the Reformers are doing.

The dragon occupies much of the right foreground of the image,
alongside the ruined building. Lettering on a large block of stone
identifies this as the pope's church in a state of decay: 'COLLAPSA
ECCLESIA PAPA'. The concept of a ruined building is a visual reference
to a similar motif in medieval imagery, especially of the birth of

Christ and the visit of the Magi, where the Christ Child and his family are shown in a ruined stable, not only to indicate the impoverished circumstances of his birth but also the way that his arrival negated the 'old' religion of Judaism. This contrast is also sometimes embodied in two women, identified as 'Synagogia' – for Judaism, often shown to be blind as a symbol of her 'refusal' to recognize the Messiah – and 'Ecclesia' – for Christianity; here the artist has adapted the idea so that the ruined building stands for the wrecked and debased Roman Church, while the maiden stands for the Reformed Church, poised in the negatively presented right-hand side of the image but about to be delivered by the heroic Christ Child/ St George to the more favourable terrain on the left. Even the tree growing outside the ruined building is attempting to direct itself away from the collapsing church.

The dragon is clearly a diabolical creature – it has humanized heads and hands but is covered in scales and fur, and the most visible neck is long and snake-like. The monster is also female – a breast or dug is visible on its body, just below the place where the spear pierces the creature. As we saw with the discussion of the dragon in the English glass panel, this presentation taps into the trope of the feminization of monsters as a way of encoding the worst, basest aspects of humanity into the body of the monster.

Our third image moves us forward in time into the seventeenth century, and presents the legend of St George's combat with a dragon on a much bigger canvas – quite literally, for the work is more than 2 metres (6 ft 7 in.) wide. In 1629–30 Peter Paul Rubens was a diplomat at the court of Charles I, the English king destined to lose his head on the block in 1649; the image shows St George with the features of the king. The identification is less immediately obvious than in the previous image, where we had the Christ Child in the guise of St George, but it is generally agreed by scholars that the saint is modelled on the king. Whether or not this reading is accurate, we can be sure that Rubens was not the first to treat St George as a form of a real person – in the previous century the German artists Albrecht Dürer and Hans Burgkmair also created works that showed identifiable people dressed as St George.[4]

The painting was described in 1630 as having been created by Rubens 'in honour of England', and he sent it home to Flanders as a remembrance of his stay in London. The painting was probably returned to England by Endymion Porter, who was Charles I's ambassador to the Spanish Netherlands, and in 1677 it was first suggested, by Roger de Piles, that the landscape and characters were specifically English. Since then it has been generally agreed that the river represents the Thames and that some of the buildings are landmarks in the London area, such as the square church tower of St Mary Overy, now Southwark Cathedral, on the left, and to the right what may be the Banqueting House in Whitehall, with a version of Westminster Abbey (before Nicholas Hawksmoor's towers were added in the following century). Further down the river, on the right of the composition, is what could be interpreted as Lambeth Palace.

The original concept of the work is centred in the area just to the left of what is now the middle section; it included St George/ Charles I speaking with the rescued princess – who, it is sometimes claimed, is modelled on Charles's consort Henrietta Maria, although there does not seem to be much of a physical resemblance to the queen. The composition was extended sometime between 1630 and 1635, with the addition of eight rectangles of canvas to the original panel, apparently so that Rubens could add two extra episodes – the mounted figure carrying a standard, on the right, and the contrast of birth and death, in the foreground. The whole process is typical of the artist's work – a number of 'expanding landscapes' are known in his *oeuvre*.

Even before the extension of the image, it seems that Rubens was intent upon creating a political allegory. The dragon plays a very small role in the work – its green colouring ensures that it blends into the verdant landscape, and it is clearly defeated, if not actually dead, at the point in the narrative that is represented. The evidence of the monster's depredations lie all around – skulls, bones and decaying flesh litters the ground. Significantly, this detritus lies *behind* the saint/king, who stands in a shaft of sunlight; a similar fall of light is cast upon figures of young children in the foreground, probably to signify hope for the prosperous future that the saint/king's victory will

Peter Paul Rubens, *Landscape with St George and the Dragon*,
1630–35, oil on canvas.

usher in. Above him two rococo angels are carrying what seem to be
a laurel crown and a palm frond (possibly a palm of martyrdom,
in recognition that the saint will give up his life for his beliefs – if
so, this is eerily prescient of the fate that would befall Charles some
two decades later).

The saint/king is clearly identified as the hero who has saved the
people from the dragon – although it is unclear in this image quite
what the dragon is meant to represent. Unlike the previous work we
considered, the dragon does not seem to be specifically identified
with Roman Catholicism; indeed, this would be unlikely given
Henrietta Maria's own Catholic background. It could be that the
dragon is a form of more generalized threats to the nation of England.
At the time of the creation of this work, the war with France and
Spain had recently ended, and it may be that the viewer is meant to
see the defeated dragon, and the havoc it has wreaked on the bodies of its victims, as a form of war; other possible identities for the
dragon include troublesome Parliamentarians – the king's period of
'personal rule' had begun in 1629 – as well as other, less specific
concepts like famine and disease.

The crowd of onlookers, most of whom seem to be peasants, appear to be rejoicing in the saint/king's victory; this tends to support the idea that this is a political allegory, with a grateful nation looking to an heroic leader. St George had certainly been used in this kind of context previously – in a fascinating recasting of 'his' gender role, a previous English monarch, Elizabeth I, had been described (in a work of 1601) as a 'valiant champion' delivering the souls of her people from the devil's power, and directly compared to the saint.[5] This presentation draws upon a well-established, late medieval aspect of the saint's cult, for he was strongly associated with ideas of authority. In fact, this identification with authority may well explain why St George came to be recognized as the patron saint of England, and indeed of so many other countries, regions and cities: he was tremendously useful to monarchs and social elites, and often employed in visual displays of power.

A good example of this kind of association is found in the civic records of the processions and pageants of the saint held annually to celebrate his feast day, known as the Ridings of St George. These took place in a number of towns in England (and also in places under English governance, such as Dublin), and were usually organized by the local guild of St George. Medieval guilds acted as a kind of social club for people with a common interest, so those who joined a guild of St George would have had a devotion to this saint. However, although the celebration of an annual Mass in honour of the saint and in memory of departed guild members was one of the main functions of a guild, it sometimes seems that this kind of overt religious practice was little more than an excuse to get together to feast, to support one another in practical ways and to impact on wider society through means that appear to be more secular than spiritual.

Religious guilds could have quite strict entry criteria, relating to social class or economic status; while the primary benefit they offered was the assurance of regular Masses said for the souls of departed members – in theory until the Second Coming of Christ – to help speed these souls' paths through Purgatory, they also offered an annual feast and an opportunity to take part in what we would now call 'networking' with merchants and local worthies. The records of the Norwich Guild of St George are very good for the late medieval period, and demonstrate that it functioned virtually as a branch of local government. The Riding was an excellent opportunity to show off the might of the city, and in particular the might of its social elite – they processed through the streets on horseback, dressed in special livery,[6] and re-enacted the combat of their patron and the dragon in a wood outside the walls. The event was rounded off by a large feast, known as the jantaculum; in 1535 this took eight days to prepare and six days to clear up afterwards so it was clearly a pretty spectacular event, and probably offered an opportunity for a display of largesse, with leftovers being doled out to the poor. This kind of 'Lady Bountiful' behaviour has a tendency to reinforce the social hierarchy, and the simple fact that St George is so frequently depicted as a mounted knight clearly labels him as part of the elite – indeed, figures of St George were routinely attacked in Revolutionary France because he was so strongly identified with the aristocracy.

Our final example of an artistic reinterpretation of St George and the dragon brings us much closer to the present day. To mark the new millennium in 2000, the artist Mark Cazalet was commissioned to create a triptych to stand on an altar in the Fraser Chapel of Manchester Cathedral; the cathedral itself is dedicated to the Virgin Mary and St Denys as well as St George. The altarpiece shows all three saints in a contemporary setting, strongly reminiscent of the actual physical location of the cathedral – St Denys is shown in a nearby shopping centre, and a woman, who seems to stand for the Virgin Mary as well as a form of Divine Wisdom, is eating a plate of chips at a café table as part of a family group with an older man (God the Father) and a younger boy (Christ).

The image of St George and the dragon, in the left panel of the triptych, is particularly striking. The saint is shown in the guise of a young black man wearing casual sportswear, including a red T-shirt with a small England flag on the breast. He is using a set of bolt cutters to free a shackled dragon, which seems cowed and pitiful rather than fierce and dangerous. The dragon here represents the creative energy of the heart of Manchester, which has been contained and suppressed by physical decay and economic blight, and the image is concerned with promoting a positive message about Christianity's potential to liberate those who suffer, and to engage with processes of urban renewal.

Cazalet informs me that the image of St George in the altarpiece is based on a portrait of the influential Jamaican musician and producer Lee 'Scratch' Perry (b. 1936), whose career since the 1960s has contributed to the development of reggae and dub, helping these styles to gain widespread recognition and acceptance around the world. While Perry has no particular link to St George that I am aware of, the artist's choice of this model has proved to be auspicious for it allows the presentation of a powerful identification of black English identity in a motif that is routinely, perhaps even unthinkingly, associated with white skin. If the saint has any historical reality it is likely that he was a native of the eastern Mediterranean, so a black St George is no more correct or incorrect than a white St George. When I first encountered the image my initial reaction was that this treatment must have been informed by the Coptic tradition of a black St George, who is identified as Ethiopia's patron saint (see the illustrations on page 46). Discussions with the artist have subsequently corrected this impression – it is a happy coincidence that the model Cazalet chose to use corresponded so closely to a well-established tradition in the cult of this saint.

By contrast, Cazalet's treatment of the dragon is, I think, unprecedented. There are one or two children's stories of St George and the dragon where the monster is presented sympathetically, but I am not aware of any visual treatments where the dragon is an object of pity, and indeed potential, rather than fear and loathing. This re-envisioning underlines the extent to which the motif of St George and the dragon is malleable, and can be used as a commentary on a wide range of issues.

The uses to which the trope can be put seem to be endless – another black St George is to be found on the cover art of the album *Confrontation* by Bob Marley and the Wailers, released in 1983, two years after Marley's death. Here St George is a dreadlocked man, clearly modelled on the reggae musician himself. Mounted on a white charger with red trappings, which invoke the colours of the flag of St

Mark Cazalet,
Trinity Reredos,
Fraser Chapel,
Manchester
Cathedral, 2001,
oil on wood,
and detail.

George and hence provide a strong link to 'conventional' imagery of the saint, the saint/musician fights a dragon which can be identified as an embodiment of 'Babylon', the term used in Rastafarianism to indicate, and reject, the corruption and greed associated with Western cultures. As with Rubens's vast canvas of Charles I, the mythology of the man merges into the mythology of the saint; the inherent malleability of St George, his dragon, and the relationship between the two, makes this transition very appealing.

Turning to literary treatments of the legend of St George, the same pattern of malleability and variation in the understandings of the saint, the dragon, and the significance of the latter's defeat, can be detected. The literary scholar Jennifer Fellows has usefully pointed out that completely developed allegory is not characteristic of medieval hagiography,[7] so during the Middle Ages the victory over the dragon is used as a device to account for the conversion of the princess, her parents and the people they rule over, rather than a means of getting a reward, such as the princess's hand in marriage, or just as an end in itself. She also notes a shift in the point in the narrative when the dragon dies – for medievals the death happens when the creature is fully under the control of the saint, as a response to the agreement to convert to Christianity; for post-medieval writers and audiences the dragon is killed in the heat of battle.

Fellows has worked extensively on Richard Johnson's *Seven Champions of Christendom* (1596–7); as we have seen, it was the most important post-Reformation treatment of the legend of St George. This work seems to have been crucial in shaping post-Reformation understandings of the saint, and instrumental in the identification of him as English-born. It can be argued that Edmund Spenser's *The Faerie Queene* has played a similar role in shaping understandings of a link between St George and England – albeit that it does not identify his place of birth. Late on in the story, in Canto x (verse 61), an aged hermit addresses the Red Crosse knight at length, including the following lines:

For thou emongst those Saints, whom thou doest see,
Shalt be a Saint, and thine owne nations frend

And Patrone: thou Saint *George* shalt called bee,
Saint *George* of mery England, the signe of victoree.

Thus we see St George acknowledged not only as the patron saint
of England but also as English himself. It is difficult to be sure quite
where or when this idea originated, but my own feeling is that it was
part of a reaction to the suppression of saints' cults at the Reformation.
St George's cult was spared the cull – despite his ahistoricity and
the fact that he was not named in the Bible – at least in part because
he was useful to the monarchy and the social elite, just as we saw
with the Ridings of St George. He moved from being a patron of
the English monarchy to the patron of the country as a whole, and
I sense that his identification as English was an attempt to explain why
he should be accepted as a patron, and also a means of a cementing
him in the nation's affections.

The process was not straightforward, however. It is notable that
George as a personal name did not become popular until the succession of Hanoverian monarchs bearing the name (they were, of
course, of German stock, and essentially imported the name). There
are instances of the use of St George in place names from the same
period, such as St George's Quay on the River Lune in Lancaster. This
important part of what was then a busy port seems to have been
given its name as a sign of patriotism rather than to denote any pre-
existing local interest in the saint, since nearby dedications to St George
post-date the naming of the quay.[8] In the same way, Matthew Boulton
(1728– 1809), coiner and manufacturer and perhaps best known as
the business partner of James Watt of steam-engine fame, placed
an image of St George and the dragon on a metal token he struck
for the Holborn innkeeper Christopher Ibbetson. The reverse stated:
'Mail & Post Coaches to all Parts of England',[9] and these words
underline the fact that by the start of the nineteenth century this
saint was a useful cipher for the nation itself in even entirely secular
contexts.

Neither Johnson nor Spenser explicitly admit that they have
manipulated the legend of St George to suit their own purposes, let
alone the national interest, but some authors have been quite open

about the revisions they have made when wielding the editorial red pen. For example, the earliest version of the life of St George in English, written by Ælfric in the late tenth century, states that he had cut material in his retelling 'in order that no tediousness be inflicted on the fastidious'.[10] Ælfric actually does not include the dragon legend – his version is a little early for that – but the principle applies equally well to versions that do contain, or indeed amount to little more than, the story of St George overcoming his monstrous foe. When it comes to the hagiography of this saint, nothing is sacred.

Thus I would argue that the modern artists and authors who have retold the story with their own variations are working in a solid tradition. In at least four children's books the knightly saint is recast as a little girl, 'Georgina', and in a rather more adult book she is the superhero 'Gina'; we should also note the French sculptor August Rodin's use of a female model, Camille Claudel (1856–1945), for a head of St George – this piece formed the basis of a bronze bust which the artist presented to the University of Glasgow in April 1906.[11] As we saw above, the cross-gendering of the saint is by no means a new departure, for in 1601 the Virgin Queen herself, Elizabeth I of England, was described in the guise of St George.

Some revisions are even more inventive. The range of products from Artisan Biscuits, based in Derbyshire, includes St George and dragon-shaped variants (they are flavoured with organic lemon curd rather than armour and scales). The story on the beautifully decorated, child-friendly box tells us that the ferocious dragon was tamed when, with St George's encouragement, the princess threw her belt around the creature's neck. The dragon then became her friend, following her everywhere, held only by a single silk thread. The children at whom the biscuits are aimed are told: 'if you can make your enemy your friend, you will have a friend for life.' This potentially radical reworking of the legend is evidently intended to encourage children to settle their differences without violence, but a deeper meaning can also be discerned, in that it tells us that St George is not a saint to be feared, shunned or vilified because of some of the less-than-politically-correct uses to which he has been put. Instead, the story

St George and the dragon biscuits, made by
Artisan Biscuits of Ashbourne.

indicates that he can be readily reclaimed and reshaped to suit new audiences and new meanings, as authors and artists have done for many centuries.

6

St George and England:
A Re-emerging Relevance?

In the years that I have spent researching St George and his cult – the better part of two decades – my understandings of the significance of this saint and the ongoing relevance of devotion to him have undergone considerable development. A series of coincidences and chance meetings, coupled with an increasing recognition of the vitality and variation associated with the saint and all that pertains to him, led me to work on him so persistently – and perhaps also the realization that very few other academic researchers were focusing on this particular cult. In part I think that this neglect is to do with over-familiarization: the ubiquity of the motif of St George and the dragon means that all too often people think they know all there is to know about the saint, when in fact their understandings are generally severely limited and sometimes plain wrong.

Furthermore, there is the significant question of what exactly a patron saint is for, especially in a largely secular society. If the principal, or even only, role is to represent a nation in public ceremonial then those who identify St George as a white, male animal-killer tend to fall one of two ways – whether or not they perceive him as an aristocrat (an identity based on his presentation as a knight, which led French revolutionaries to destroy images of him with particular relish). Many English people are profoundly uncomfortable with having a national representative who is perceived as being unable to represent so many elements of the population, and they are often uncertain about celebration of national identity on any level beyond pride in sporting achievements. Flying the flag of St George is sometimes read as a xenophobic act, and attempts to mark St George's Day in religious, community or educational settings can attract criticism when they are identified as seeking to promote a divisive, even racist figure. By contrast, there are those who are very happy to promote the concept of St George as a white, male animal-killer, and only too willing to use this motif to their own ends. For example, members of right-wing organizations tend to be very resistant to seeing St George as anything other than a 'true-born Englishman' with all that stereotype conjures up: they can struggle to accept him as a Palestinian Christian let alone accept a devotion that is shared with Islam.

The people who tend to fall into the first camp – those uncomfortable with the concept of St George as a national symbol – can find it hard to separate the saint and his universal cult from the associations with imperialism and jingoism that have developed, even though they form only a very minor element in the overall picture. My experience of the cult of St George in other nations suggests this unease around St George is peculiar to England. A number of European countries have deeply problematic legacies of colonial activity, but no one else seems to place feelings of guilt onto their patron saint in quite the way that the English do. As we have seen, St George functions as either a national or local patron in a wide range of countries, regions and towns across Europe and beyond, and the fact that he is honoured with such unbridled enthusiasm in so many parts of the world tends to demonstrate that there is a role for patron saints to play that can transcend fears of offending others, just as patriotism need not imply a belief that a particular nation must be shown to triumph over 'lesser' places.

Although discussion of St George in England still has to take place in the context of a corrective of misunderstandings and concerns, I am aware of an increasing level of interest in him, both in 'serious' academic study and at popular levels; to some extent this seems to be a reflection of the extent to which his ubiquity, usefulness and multicultural credentials are coming to be appreciated more fully. Some of the most interesting discussions I have had about St George have been with English artists, poets and dramatists. They are working in a long line of creative people who have been inspired by the saint and his mythology, most obviously the visual reworkings of his legend presented by the Pre-Raphaelites and writers such as Richard Johnson; outside the Anglophone world there is an equally strong tradition of artistic attention to the saint and his dragon. Each has a habit of turning up in some less obvious art forms as well as visual imagery and performance.

One example is in the *oeuvre* of the Catalan architect Antoni Gaudí, who was very interested in dragons: he created a large mosaic dragon at Parc Güell in Barcelona and he made a reference to Ladon, the dragon of classical myth who guarded the entrance to the Garden of the Hesperides, in the gates for the estate of Finca Güell. Furthermore, the design of the Casa Batlló in Barcelona may well have been inspired to some extent by the legend of St George; under the name Sant Jordi, he is the patron saint of Catalonia (see the image on page 49) so Gaudí surely will have been aware of the story. The Casa Batlló is a remodelling of a pre-existing building. It features a scale-like motif in the mosaic facing of the sandstone facade, and bone-like pillars in the balustrades of the lower balconies, while the equivalent features on the top storeys strongly resemble the upper part of a human skull. There are a number of theories about the basis of the design of the house, including Monet's water lilies and a Harlequin's hat, but a frequent interpretation is that the roof is a dragon, surmounting the remains of its many victims. St George, the dragon's vanquisher, is represented by a small turret with a cross motif – this can be read as the saint's sword, piercing the creature below.

On one level it would be reassuring to be able securely to pin down St George as an inspiration for Gaudí – a specific reference in a notebook kept by the artist or a letter sent by him would offer a kind of security – but in many ways the lack of certainty is quite liberating. The possibilities that are opened up by the absence of definitiveness give space for reappraisal and reimaginings. This trend can be detected within a number of contemporary artists' approaches to St George – they tend to treat him and his legend with a refreshing freedom, crossing cultural and emotional boundaries in ways that profoundly challenge the mental image that so many English people have of the saint.

Casa Batlló, Barcelona, redesigned by Antoni Gaudí in 1904.

The work of composer and performer Joe Townsend is a good example of this broad approach.[1] He is leading an ongoing project in partnership with Opera North and Leeds University, which has lasted more than five years so far, based on the songs of peoples who identify St George as their patron saint. The saint is presented as a weary figure – he is invoked by so many and made responsible for so much. Traditional folk song, such as Lebanese chants, is blended with the blogs of soldiers in Iraq, and Townsend also draws upon the tradition of mummers' plays, especially the aspect of wordplay, and the connected style of *teatro bufo*, used most famously by the Italian playwright and activist Dario Fo. An ad-lib comment credited to Fo states that St George was sold by crafty Genoese merchants to the unsuspecting English as their patron saint; Townsend was inspired by this idea and extends the crossing of cultural boundaries by linking the saint to secular heroes of Northern and Eastern Europe who slay dragons and rescue maidens, to the Slavic Dobrynya Nikitich and to the Romanian Iovan Iorgovan. The latter is usually identified as a form of the classical Hercules; Townsend is moving beyond established convention here, and although there are some similarities of theme – Iovan's dragon, like St George's, is described as a source of pestilence – there are many more differences. For example, the rescued princess is revealed to be Iovan's sister – Townsend informs me that this reflects a theme of potential incest that is found in Romanian epic more generally – while in Russian tradition Dobrynya marries a woman entirely separate from the maiden he rescues, one who is identified as a female warrior in her own right.

The performance, which has been described by one participant as 'vignettes with music – or possibly music with vignettes', also invokes a range of paradigms beyond the legend of the hero and the dragon. These include the 'St George Defence' – an unorthodox opening move in chess which was most famously used by the first English grandmaster, Tony Miles, to defeat the reigning world champion Anatoly Karpov, a Russian, at a European competition in 1980. This unexpected and bizarre victory can be read as a form of the motif of 'plucky little England' standing up to the might of the Soviets during the Cold War, and also perhaps plays on the (self-defined) ideal of English eccentricity and resourcefulness. Townsend similarly references the significance of a painting of St George and the dragon, by the Italian Renaissance artist Uccello, to the main character in the 2001 novel *Rot (Red)* by the German writer Uwe Timm. *Rot* draws in turn on images, including a hero and dragon, in the Swiss psychiatrist Carl Gustav Jung's illustrated diary *The Red Book* (written between 1914 and 1930). Townsend commented to me that synchronicity is very significant within the performance, and this is underlined by the simultaneous presentation of different aspects of the work: towards the end of the piece a speech that plays on the idea of the saint as a figure of xenophobia is essentially drowned out by music which demonstrates that multicultural musical collaboration can offer hope for the re-emergence of St George as a unifying figure. In the same way the saint's identification with the military is a strong feature of the work, with commentary on the use of St George as a tool of recruitment in the Crusades juxtaposed with his personification for part of the performance by an Iraqi Kurd in a prison cell.

Although Townsend arguably focuses primarily on the cross-cultural connections of St George, some artists have chosen to

Paolo Uccello, *St George and the Dragon*, c. 1455–60, oil on canvas.

comment more directly on the vexed role he plays in the concept of Englishness itself. The contemporary playwright and poet John Constable, whose work is closely identified with the London Borough of Southwark, includes a clear statement on this issue in his major work *The Southwark Mysteries*,[2] first performed in Southwark Cathedral to mark the new millennium and revived in 2010:

> Then as George came down in History
> he fell in with bad company
> they dressed him up in Gordon's bigots' clothes,
>
> with their Roast Beefs and Bully Boys
> a-marching making mighty noise
> to George's Fields to bloody Patrick's nose.
>
> And George was all too willing
> to take their thirty shilling
> for to go a Dragon-killing for their sluttish English Rose,

and the Mob made him the stronger
dinged the Dragons with his donger
then he chopped 'em up and fed 'em to the crows.

Now George, seeing the error
of his ways did flee in terror he
took refuge in the hospice of St Mary Overie,

where Sister Martha did receive him
nursed him through his gruesome grieving
then they set about the healing

of the Dragon
slain in the name of England
St George and Liberty.

This is an excerpt from 'George and the Dragon Rap', which is performed within the play by a group of mummers and accompanied
by a stylized dumbshow in which St George progresses from Christian
martyr, through dragon-killing Crusader and icon of English national-
ism, to repentance for the evil he has done. Constable's stage directions
indicate that the rap ends with St George weeping over the butchered
body of the dragon; both the monster and the saint are then washed
and healed by women, the Sisters of Redcross and characters based
on St Martha and St Margaret. The latter are assisted by a form of
St Michael – all three have dragon-slaying legends of their own in
traditional Christian hagiography.

Constable tells me that his interest in St George is wide-ranging.
Like Townsend, he is attracted to the idea of the saint being trapped
by expectations and accretions, and thinks of him 'wasting away
in his rusty armour'.[3] However, in this context the saint is a shape-
shifter who plays a key part in the vision of reconciliation, transformation and urban regeneration that informs *The Southwark Mysteries*.
The negative shapes into which St George has been shifted are set
out in the rap. First, he is identified with the Gordon Riots, anti-
Catholic protests in 1780 which are considered to have been the

most destructive episode of urban disorder in eighteenth-century London – among other aspects, they effectively destroyed the career of John Wilkes, mentioned in the last chapter as the radical politician whose imprisonment had led to the St George's Fields Massacre in 1768 as he led troops against 'King Mob' and apparently instructed the soldiers to fire on rioters. On this occasion he was identified with the 'establishment', as part of the defence of the Bank of England. The mention of 'Liberty' as an unworthy cause of the dragon's death strongly recalls the shouts of 'No Liberty, No King!' ascribed to the rebels of St George's Fields. Second, Constable extends the theme of embodiment of belief in saintly form by identifying Catholicism as St Patrick in opposition to a 'Protestant' St George. This plays on the personification of a nation in its patron saint – an anonymous, scurrilous poem published in 1800 used St Patrick as a form of Ireland in opposition to St George as a form of England,[4] so there is a good lineage for this kind of idea.

Constable's reimagining of St George is deeply rooted in the history, imagery and urban landscape of Southwark; he is not alone in identifying the saint as a powerful and multifaceted symbol of the borough. One example is the work of Mental Fight Club, a user-led creative force exploring issues around mental illness, wellness and recovery, which takes inspiration from Ben Okri's epic poem *Mental Fight* (first published in 1999).[5] They currently meet weekly in the crypt of St George's Church for a range of creative activities and discussions; the location is a happy coincidence, for St George was chosen as one of the patrons of the group well before they started to use this physical space. However, it could be said that it would have been difficult to avoid St George in Southwark, for there are nine sites in the borough within a ten-minute walk of this church that are specifically linked through name or imagery with either the saint or dragons. The founder of Mental Fight Club, Sarah Wheeler & Thomas Tobias, tells me that she became interested in the saint before she discovered that he is identified both with healing in general and with psychiatric issues in particular.[6] The realization of this particularly salient aspect of the saint reinforced her perception that he is a symbol of great power, both in Southwark and further afield. A phrase that the artist Nicola Moss used seems to encapsulate this aspect of his appeal: the motif of St George and the dragon 'is full of potency . . . [it] gives meaning to people's lives that are seemingly chaotic or in an intolerable state'.[7]

Mental Fight Club uses St George and his dragon in a range of ways, but the high point of their year is clearly the communal festivities for St George's Day, which in 2013 featured parading dragon puppets, dance, poetry, a tea party, illustrated talks and a video animation. The day incorporated a focus on Chinese cultural activities, and actively sought to include a sense of St George as a universal figure as well as a motif of Englishness and a healer. These kinds of inclusive public events have the potential to play a significant role in dismantling the political and cultural unease that the figure attracts because of his modern association with 'empire' and authority. This approach identifies the saint as a figure who can act as a key to the multifaceted nature of English identity – crossing cultures, genders, classes and states of being – due to the complexity of the figure and the ways in which different layers of meaning have been associated with him over time and place.

This understanding chimes with John Constable's discussion of the link between St George and England in *The Southwark Mysteries*: he sees this as complex and problematic, even presenting the saint as a form of the traitor Judas, having his head turned to an ill end for the proverbial 30 pieces of silver. Yet Constable strongly asserts the idea of the saint – and Englishness – as both redeemable and worthy of redemption. St George weeps over the body of the dragon; the true regret he demonstrates ties into Constable's identification of the dragon itself as a form of creative energy that can be harnessed to good ends, for that which is 'evil' and 'wrong' can be reimagined as 'positive' and 'affirming'. The rehabilitated St George can work with, rather than against, the revived monster to the benefit of all. Constable stresses that within his work he presents dragon-healing and dragon-slaying as a false dichotomy; both binding and loosing are needed to achieve psychic wholeness, and boundaries are needed to channel and focus creativity. The girdling of the dragon – an image that also seems to have appealed to Uccello (see page 125) – is a crucial part of this concept, representing for Constable the control of the self which permits full actualization.

Returning to the theme of St George and Englishness, a less hopeful tone is adopted by Ron Scowcroft in his poem 'Bitter at The George'[8] of 2013:

> He sees it all in red and white,
> leans at the barmaid,
> stabs the air with the studied
> emphasis of the one-too-many.
> *They've even stole our saint.*
>
> And this is his rightful place:
> twilight settling through leaded windows,
> ersatz knights, rampant dragons
> and the hiss of gas from the brassed-up
> mockery of an ancient fire.
>
> There are tide lines of bitter
> in his glass, angry gulps of froth.
> You think to mention al-Khidr,
> the lineage to Libya,
> those who don't drink from the same cup
> but it's a line you can't cross.
> He'll skewer you with the way he sees it
> every time.

Scowcroft eloquently reflects the extent to which this saint is embedded almost thoughtlessly into English culture – not least in the names of pubs – on the basis of what is often a very limited understanding of the history of his cult. He too easily appears to be no more than an irrelevant figure of past romance, and this impression conspires with the imperialist overtones of works such as *Where the Rainbow Ends* – a play and novelization that was tremendously popular in the first half of the twentieth century, and was still being staged in the 1960s – which strongly identifies the saint as 'English of the English' in a context of racism, anti-Semitism and the unworthiness of the lower classes. The net result is a palpable unease around the saint, even in those who know enough about his cult to be able to challenge misunderstandings, and it can be a daunting job to unpick the layers of meaning within the myth.

The complexity of St George's position in English consciousness is certainly tangible in the recent experience of Manchester Cathedral in relation to the imagery used by Mark Cazalet in the *Trinity Reredos* (see page 115). This work has been displayed in the Fraser chapel from its installation in 2001 without apparently attracting any negative comment, but in 2010 the cathedral commissioned processional giants based on the images of St George and the dragon used in this work, and newspaper coverage of the unveiling of the figures led to some deeply unfortunate attention which extended to hate mail and even death threats.

Cazalet had chosen to show St George as a young black man in sportswear, freeing a cowed and shackled dragon which represents the potential of urban regeneration – an idea that also informs *The Southwark Mysteries'* envisioning of St George and the dragon. There were many complaints about the presentation of a black St George, most of which assumed – incorrectly – that this was an attempt to make him more 'politically correct'. In fact the contested image would have been perfectly authentic as a representation of him as the patron saint of Ethiopia, and St George was portrayed by the black South African actor Wela Mbusi in the Royal Opera House production of Harrison Birtwistle's opera *Down by the Greenwood Side* in 2009.[9] It therefore forms an entirely appropriate commentary on the malleability and applicability of this saint.

However, this was not the perception of the angry correspondents who wrote to the cathedral and the national media in protest about the processional giants – as far as they were concerned, this was a deliberate subversion of an inviolable symbol of white English identity that aimed to undermine its status and attack white people themselves. This kind of extreme response is undoubtedly a minority view, but I think it is likely that a number of people in the local community would have had concerns about the presentation of any form of St George,

(Top row) Crown (1902) of Edward VII featuring Benedetto Pistrucci's design of St George and the dragon; (bottom row) crown (1935) of George V, featuring Percy Metcalfe's design of St George and the dragon.

whether white or black, in a public procession, since they associate this saint with a version of England that makes them profoundly uncomfortable.

The proliferation of images of St George overcoming the dragon on British coinage may have some element of responsibility for this unease, for it provides a concrete connection between the saint and the ruling elite of the country – as the image here shows, the motif is inevitably paired with the profile of the monarch, so that it forms the reverse of what has at times been a literal token of imperialism. The upper coin is the 'standard' form of St George and the dragon – used on sovereigns and crowns from 1816 – in a design by Benedetto

Pistrucci with the saint depicted as a Roman-style soldier overcoming a supine dragon. The second coin forms quite a contrast – this is the 'rocking horse crown' of 1935, minted to mark the silver jubilee of George V; it was the first truly commemorative coin issued by the Royal Mint.[10] The design, by Percy Metcalfe, is markedly different to Pistrucci's, and the king is said to have objected that the saint's straightened knee marked him out as a very poor horseman – the jocular term 'rocking horse crown' may perhaps refer to the fact that this style of riding is more inclined to get the rocking motion going effectively on a toy horse than it is to persuading a real horse to assist the fight with a dragon. Metcalfe's St George is clearly a medieval knight, and obviously linked to England by the clear frontal presentation of his shield with its St George's cross, and records from the Royal Mint Museum indicate that the coinage committee was split on whether or not to commission this design. A St George was required, as a tribute to the monarch's name (just as with the naming of St George's Quay in Lancaster) – but did the form have to be quite so radical? Looking back from 80 years later we can perhaps appreciate that the lively Art Deco style marks out the time of its creation just as much as the engraved date – it is much more evocative than the 'conventional' design which had been in use for more than a century. Metcalfe makes a far greater feature of the dragon's details – the barbed tongue, curved claws and sinuous tail – than is possible in Pistrucci's more compact treatment: perhaps the sole feature they have in common is the snake-like neck.

Echoes of Pistrucci's design can be found in a cast bronze art medal created by Nicola Moss, though she takes the concept of the struggle between the saint and dragon in a rather different direction by offering a feminist reinterpretation of the legend. The obverse shows a naked and sinewy St George on horseback – the horse too is bare, with no saddle or bridle, and it is notable that Pistrucci's St George appears to be naked apart from his helmet and flowing mantle, and also rides without the benefit of saddlery. Here the similarities end, though. In Moss's piece a large lizard-like dragon is effectively wrapped around the horse, not trampled underneath it – heads and tails seem to be intertwined in a clear deviation from the

Nicola Moss, *St George and the Dragon*; *George and the Maiden*, 1986, bronze.

form usually adopted by medieval images, where only the dragon's tail interacts directly with the horse, wrapping itself around one of the creature's trampling legs (a version of this is found in Metcalfe's design, where the monster's tail is coiled round one of the horse's hooves). Significantly, no spear or sword is visible, in clear contrast to the representations on the coins, and virtually all other treatments of the theme. The lively design used by Moss is arresting in itself, but the reverse of the piece is even more surprising. The naked maiden has grown bored of waiting to be rescued and decides to do the job herself, cutting off her long hair to draw strength and gain her independence. Long hair on a woman traditionally functions in Western art to symbolize both overt femininity and also wanton female sexuality, and the act of cutting it off is very powerful as a rejection of both these labels. For me it recalls the biblical story of Samson, who lost his strength when his hair was cut, but here we seem to have something very different happening – perhaps because the protagonist is a woman, or perhaps because she has made a deliberate decision and administers the barbering herself – in both senses this is the opposite of Samson's emasculation.

Moss tells me that she identifies St George as 'a landmark in our cultural soul[,] a perfect expression of the struggles we face in life that inevitably transform us'.[11] She explains that she generally tries to avoid being influenced by other people's usage or interpretation of symbolic imagery; this must be well-nigh impossible when it comes to the ubiquitous figure of St George, but it certainly seems that she contrived to come up with a new approach to this well-trodden subject. Looking back from a quarter of a century later, Moss states that she was aware that what she was making could be seen as controversial, and she was challenging viewers on two fronts. Most obviously the maiden is shown as active rather than as a passive agent – no waiting around to be rescued for her. Furthermore, St George is bridling the dragon rather than killing it, and, as Moss sees it, taming the dragon in order that it should serve, perhaps in the way that a horse is broken to the bridle. As with the work of Joe Townsend, Jung's discussion of archetypes has been influential on Nicola Moss. The motif of nakedness evokes a sense of primal innocence, but this is cut across by the use of the bridle and the scissors – an aspect of control and liberation is evoked, which seems to fit with Constable's shamanic vision of binding and loosing. Significantly, the maiden is not on the primary surface of the medal but on what the artist describes as an 'inner plain' – perhaps representing Moss's own inner world. The fish on the left of the image, inhabiting the watery curtain of the medal's surface, sees her revealed and perhaps is even surprised, anticipating the human viewer's own response.

Moss commented to me that the story of St George and the dragon can be understood as 'a divine blueprint or symbol relating to the struggle and transformation from matter to spirit', and this powerful theme of transcendence is one that clearly appeals to a number of devotees. There is a fine balance of elements in this legend – the human and the monster, the male and the female, the chaste and the sexual, the flesh and the soul. Artists, writers and performers continue to find inspiration in this eternal story, and there seems to be little likelihood that the stream of new interpretations and reworkings will run dry.

Conclusion:
Where Next for St George?

We English,[1] a portfolio of photographs by Simon Roberts depicting people at leisure out of doors in various parts of England from August 2007 to September 2008, contains an intriguing image relating to the cult of St George. 'St George's Day Pageant, Scarborough Castle, North Yorkshire, 26th April 2008' shows the ruined keep of Scarborough Castle amid green lawns, set against a grey sea merging into a grey sky. A handful of visitors populate the foreground, and a car park occupies the middle distance, but there is little else in the detail to draw the eye. In particular, there is no element of pageantry, and no sign of St George. The pages of notes at the back of the book offer little help to the reader: the photographer provides some thoughtful notes on many of the images in this collection, but this one is passed over completely.

When I encountered this conundrum I was very conscious of the furore at Manchester Cathedral caused by the presentation of a black St George as a processional giant. I realized that the absence of St George, and any obvious pageantry, from this image could be interpreted as a rather good motif of the widespread English unease around the figure of their patron saint.[2] We know he exists in some sense – as a concept if not as a historical reality – but we are not quite sure what to do with him. On the whole he is safer tucked away out of sight. Pageantry of St George, such as there is in England, tends to be either low key or a source of embarrassment and controversy.

During research for this book I have spent time viewing online video footage of St George's Day parades, such as the one that has taken place for a number of years at Sandwell in the West Midlands, England; it is notable that issues around funding and the threat of withdrawal of formal civic support are often a feature of the discourse that surrounds these events. The political unease can extend as far as counter-demonstrations, especially where there is a perception that the parade could be used as a platform for the promotion of a national-ist xenophobic agenda. Admittedly, St George is wheeled out for the occasional national event where, in company with his dragon, he can be used as a simple motif of good versus evil to encourage fair play – the most recent example I am aware of is the opening ceremony, held at Wembley Stadium, of the Euro '96 football championships – he was noticeably absent from the London Olympics of 2012, and this too may speak of an ongoing suspicion of what St George represents. The BBC continues to fight shy of giving his feast day any coverage beyond modest airings on local radio stations. There is no English equivalent of the large-scale communal celebrations of the saint that take place in a range of locations around the world – the annual Ducasse festival, or Doudou, in Mons, Belgium, is just one example of the potency of St George as a symbol of civic pride, where he is apparently uncontested as a positive symbol.

Despite this continuing English disquiet St George does man-age to infiltrate himself into a wide variety of situations, from the highbrow to the populist. He is frequently found on currency, on commercial insignia, in the names of schools, parks and a range of public buildings. This naming tendency arises even more obviously outside England – there are many towns and villages in Europe and North America, hotels, markets, airports, more schools and even a university (in Grenada) which are called after him. A Beanie Baby bear of St George could be purchased as part of a range of patron saint soft toys in 2008 – though in truth it seemed to be modelled on King Arthur as the figure was crowned, dressed in mail and had a badge of the sword in the stone, with no sign of the red cross device. Another Beanie Baby bear, called George, is resplendent in red fur and has a small badge of the flag of St George on his chest – he is sold with the overt acknowledgement that he stands for England, though whether people in Ethiopia, Georgia and a number of other

Simon Roberts, 'St George's Day Pageant, Scarborough Castle, North Yorkshire, 26th April 2008', photograph published in *We English*.

countries who claim St George as their patron would recognize him as 'theirs' too is probably open to question.

Google tend to modify their search engine home page in response to the significance of specific dates, and it has published some lovely commentaries on St George, especially in cartoon form in recent years. In 2008 he could be seen charging over a hill on his white horse to deal with a dragon which had set light to the second 'o' in Google's logo. The following year they were on more friendly terms, with St George, again in full armour, kneeling to present a bunch of flowers to a 'lady' dragon looking coyly to one side as she stood on a small balcony on top of the 'l' in the logo, rather in the manner of the famous scene in Shakespeare's *Romeo and Juliet*. The designer was clearly aware of 23 April as Shakespeare's (probable) birthday and death date, but one wonders if there was also a commentary on the tradition of presenting the monster as female; if so, this is definitely a subversion of the intention to highlight the evil and depravity of the dragon through her gender role!

In 2014 I witnessed for the first time an attempt by a large supermarket to cash in on St George's Day, using his image – or a version of it – to promote English beer. In fact Sainsbury's chose a rather strange version – there is no identifying dragon, and the presence of a beard, though not unparalleled, is decidedly unusual, for his patronage of the Scouting movement is linked to an identification of him as a young man able to defend the young. In some accounts of his life he was only 23 when he died, conjuring up a very different concept to the mature, bearded figure shown here. Just as the Beanie Baby bear of St George seems to have been influenced by King Arthur, is it at least possible that the designer of this image was thinking of a crusader? The presence of the helm under the arm, rather than on the figure's head, does allow for a sense that this is a cavalryman taking home his shopping.

Perhaps this move by Sainsbury's is indicative of a softening of English attitudes to their patron – and the number of opinion pieces in the print and online media on St George's Day in the same year does seem to indicate at least a willingness to engage with questions around who he was and what he could represent as a national patron. It is also

Roundel advertising a St George's Day beer promotion.

Svetlana Petrova, *Feeding Your Winged Cat*, 2012,
photograph after Paolo Uccello.

notable that he is recognized to offer commercial value beyond his
apparent endorsement of beer. The makers of replica England football (soccer) kit claim that the 'new metallic weave that gives the shirt
a distinctive shine [is] inspired by the armour worn by St George,
the English patron saint'.[3] How could a patriotic England fan resist?

Elsewhere we can find well-known imagery of St George himself reimagined to quite startling effect, including a version of Uccello's
St George and the Dragon (as seen on page 125). The dragon is replaced
by a huge ginger cat bearing the wings, complete with military-style
roundels, of the original fifteenth-century monster. This work, *Feeding
Your Winged Cat*, is by the Russian artist Svetlana Petrova, who has
been inspired to integrate photographs of her cat Zarathustra into
pre-existing images, ranging from Old Masters to contemporary
works (her image of a giant cat lying on top of a tank of formaldehyde
that contains a dead shark – Damien Hirst's *The Impossibility of Death
in the Mind of Someone Living* – is particularly compelling). Petrova's
revisionist approach is indicative of the extent to which modern technology allows artistic boundaries to be pushed, but it also sits in a

fine tradition of reinterpretations of St George. The saint is feeding the cat, not attacking it – he holds out a small piece of bloody meat on the end of his lance, which the cat is about to devour. The princess is the owner of the animal, not its potential prey, and she is asking for St George's advice on ways to help it lose weight (it is too heavy to fly, according to Petrova's brief commentary), rather than relying upon him to rescue her from its ravening maws.

This reimagining of the combat as a more peaceful encounter is certainly unusual, but the realignment of the dynamics within the triangle of hero–dragon–maiden has been attempted several times in recent years. In one of her most celebrated poems, again inspired by Uccello's work, the poet U. A. Fanthorpe maintains the basic legendary relationship between the three protagonists, but makes it clear that she senses there is more going on under the surface of this Renaissance painting.[4] Fanthorpe's maiden is less than impressed with her 'rescuer', stating that she 'quite took to the dragon . . . you could see all his equipment / At a glance.' The feeling of attraction was not mutual – Fanthorpe's dragon asks: 'Why should my victim be so / Unattractive as to be inedible [?]'. St George, meanwhile, asks both the princess and the dragon (and perhaps also the reader): 'Don't / You want to carry out the roles / That sociology and myth have designed for you?', indicating that the poet had a clear sense of the extent to which she was subverting the standard reading of the legend. An element of sexualization of the story can also be detected in Nicola Moss's art medal (shown on p. 134), which shows the maiden rescuing herself without any help from St George, cutting off her own long hair to symbolize both a loss of innocence and a reappraisal of sensuousness.

The sometime performance artist David Pedder has told me about an even more radical reworking.[5] During the late 1990s he was part of a group of actors and musicians who created a show to be presented at village fiestas in Spain, featuring St George's dragon ridden by a flute-playing Baba Yaga, the witch of Russian folklore, attacking a castle rebuilt for each show from bed bases and other detritus scavenged from the local tip. The show always concluded with the burning of the castle and a fireworks display, spectacular to a greater or lesser extent according to the budget that the village had available. The diverse group of ethnicities and cultures in the performance troupe (including English, Irish, Dutch and Catalan) found that they could coalesce around the motif of the hero and the dragon, and they chose to present a subversion of it. The performances were always held at night, and in the struggle between light and dark the darkness would always win – although the pyrotechnics could perhaps be interpreted as a way of showing that the forces of chaos and wilderness (personified as Baba Yaga and the dragon) could harness light to their own ends. What is really striking is that the myth enacted in these shows excluded St George entirely – his absence was a commentary on the extent to which he is present in so many contexts. If he was represented at all in the performance it was within the structure of the 'establishment' castle, destroyed at the conclusion. Another interpretation is that St George was subsumed into Baba Yaga – the Christian knight had become a powerful female witch, showing the unremarked side of an apparently familiar coin. The performance troupe realized how powerful the hero and dragon could be if they were teamed together rather than presented in opposition to one another – a combination which would be capable of great evil as well as great good.

This multiplicity of approaches to St George is testament to the power of this totemic figure – he is able to encompass all these meanings and many more. His Islamic analogue, Al-Khidr, has been described as 'human, angelic, mundane and celestial' and it is claimed that 'he talks the languages of all people';[6] effectively, everything you could ask for in a patron is covered. I feel that when the breadth and richness of his cult is fully appreciated it becomes apparent that this observation is also true of St George himself. This diversity is an impressive achievement for any mythic figure, let alone one that has attracted so much controversy. I close with the hope that this book will assist in the process of re-evaluation and reappraisal, and help to establish that England can justifiably celebrate its status as part of a family of nations and peoples who find St George a meaningful and powerful patron who can be reimagined in manifold ways.

REFERENCES

Introduction: 'God is Great but Not Like St George'

1 Marlène Kanaan, 'Legends, Places and Traditions Relating to the Cult of Saint George in Lebanon', *ARAM*, XX (2008), pp. 203–19. *ARAM* is a periodical published by the ARAM Society for Syro-Mesopotamian Studies. This volume is the proceedings of the ARAM conference on 'Iconography and Mythology of the Prophet Elijah, St George and al-Khodor in the Syrian Orient', 4–6 July 2006, Oxford.

2 'St George', www.copticchurch.net, accessed 6 December 2013.

3 For the purposes of this book the term 'Holy Land' is used to denote modern confines of Israel and Palestine, and no political or geographical judgement is intended or should be inferred.

4 'Horus on horseback', www.louvre.fr, accessed 10 June 2014.

5 St George is often decried on the grounds of lack of historical authenticity – admittedly a hard claim to refute – and as a non-native saint, although this second charge can also be levelled against St Edmund (German), St Augustine (Roman) and St Alban (possibly Roman). St Edward the Confessor was certainly English-born, although his claim to be a good national patron saint is rather undermined by a patchy track record as a monarch of the country – his failure to secure the succession to the throne led directly to the Norman Conquest. A similarly problematic reign dogs the claims of St Edmund too – while St Cuthbert, St Alban and St Augustine are arguably rather too 'Christian' to be able to represent the diverse society that comprises England. St George has none of these disadvantages – and I would argue that his lack of historical authenticity is actually part of his power, for he can be endlessly reconstructed to suit a variety of needs.

6 St George is described in these terms when his presence is successfully wished for, due to his 'splendid chivalry to maidens in distress' and his 'ripping way' of killing dragons, in Clifford Mills, *Where the Rainbow Ends* (London, 1932), p. 67.

1 St George: A Reappraisal for a Multicultural Age

1 Readers who wish to find out what I think on this issue, and why, are invited to consult *St George: Hero, Martyr and Myth* (Stroud, 2000; new edn 2005), especially the first chapter.
2 Luis Erlanger, quoted in Loretta Chao, 'A Soap Set in the Favelas', *Wall Street Journal*, 1 November 2012.
3 It is worth noting that there is no 'original' or urtext of the life of St George: even the earliest surviving legends seem to be copying something else.
4 The phrase is attributed to Thomas Arundel (Archbishop of Canterbury, 1396–1414) at the Synod of Cambridge. This meeting of clerics was a key element in the usurpation of the crown by Henry Bolingbroke (later Henry iv) from Richard ii, and this fits with the assertion that a strong interest in St George was a marker of a 'good' or 'true' English medieval monarch – something that really came to the fore in the Wars of the Roses. Richard ii was notable for his relative lack of interest in this saint – perhaps his neglect of visible connection with this significant figure of authority was part of his undoing.

2 Misrepresentations and Reinventions: St George across Continents and Cultures

1 The identification of St George as the champion of the Virgin Mary – usually under the sobriquet 'Our Lady's Knight' – formed a significant part of his cult in late medieval England. It is discussed in detail in Samantha Riches, *St George: Hero, Martyr and Myth* (Stroud, 2000; new edn 2005).
2 We noted in chapter One that it was not until the eleventh century that St George started to become identified as a dragon-slayer. Up until this point his cult was predicated on the saint as a suffering martyr – and this identity continued to have resonance in England until the Reformation. Meanwhile in many traditions of Christianity, and perhaps particularly the Orthodox variants, he is still celebrated as a martyr just as much as he is venerated as a dragon-slayer.
3 John Pinkerton, *A General Collection of the Best and Most Interesting Voyages in All Parts of the World: Many of Which are Now First Translated into English: Digested on a New Plan*, vol. xv (London, 1814), p. 186; 'Που φυλακίστηκε ο Αγιος Γεώργιος', www.youtube.com, accessed 10 June 2013.
4 Marlène Kanaan, 'Legends, Places and Traditions Relating to the Cult of Saint George in Lebanon', *ARAM*, xx (2008), pp. 203–19, at p. 207.
5 Pinkerton, *A General Collection* (London, 1811), vol. x, p. 477.
6 Kanaan, 'Legends, Places and Traditions', p. 212.
7 Personal communication with Dan Koski, November 2012.

8 The devotion of the confraternity (almost exactly contemporary with the founding of the Order of the Garter in England) roughly translates as 'God and St George', though perhaps with rather more emphasis on fealty to St George in Picard than in English.

9 The date of Trinity Sunday is set by Easter, which is, of course, a moveable feast, so the time difference between St George's Day and Trinity Sunday is variable. In 2012 Trinity Sunday fell on 3 June, so the *Lumeçon* was enacted some six weeks after 23 April.

10 An excellent overview of Georgian history is provided in Donald Rayfield, *Edge of Empires: A History of Georgia* (London, 2012). Chapter Twelve is ominously entitled 'Fratricide': this gives some sense of the bloodthirsty nature of the events recounted in the text, where eye-gouging, castration and defenestration are repeatedly mentioned. The episodes referred to above appear within a few pages of one another: p. 208 (*c.* 1635–9), p. 212 (1683), p. 195 (December 1623).

3 St George and the Natural World: A Symbol of Fertility

1 Quotations from the *Bury Pace-egging Play* and *The Peace Egg* are taken from the versions published in Eddie Cass and Steve Roud, *An Introduction to the English Mummers' Play* (London, 2002), pp. 98–107.

2 Despite the significance of Johnson's and Kirke's narratives of St George, we should be aware that there is little in the way of wholesale borrowings. The theme of resurrection, which is so strong in the mumming tradition, is played out in quite a different way in the *Seven Champions*, with an orange tree rather than a doctor providing two cures for the hero. After the first assault on the dragon, when the saint's spear is shattered, he retreats into the shade cast by the tree. The monster is kept away by the 'pretious vertue' of the tree and St George recovers himself sufficiently to sally forth and attack it again, using his sword, 'Ascalon'. This time his armour is burst open by the strength of the venom which issues from the body of the beast, but the juice of an orange, conveniently falling to the ground within his reach, helps the hero's recovery, and he is then able to pierce the dragon's side under its wing and stab it through the heart.

3 St George as the Virgin's champion is noted briefly in chapter Two; for a more detailed account see Samantha Riches, *St George: Hero, Martyr and Myth* (Stroud, 2000, new edn 2005).

4 Mall Hiiemäe, 'Some Possible Origins of St George's Day Customs and Beliefs', *Folklore*, 1 (1996). Available online at www.folklore.ee/folklore, accessed 21 November 2014. Discussion in this chapter of traditions in Estonia and nearby areas, including those of the Setu people, is derived from Hiiemäe's article: attempts to contact the author have proved unsuccessful.

5 C. Sisan and K. Sisan, eds, *The Oxford Book of Medieval English Verse* (Oxford, 1973), p. 384.

6 Personal communication with Katja Fält, January 2012.
7 Garth Cartwright, 'St George and the Roma People', www.
   stgeorgesdayproject.org.uk, 2 September 2012 (an article written
   for an educational website aimed at schools). The same author provides
   a less positive account of the same event in his travelogue *Princes
   Amongst Men: Travels with Gypsy Musicians* (London, 2005), pp. 1–5.

4 St George as a Saint of Water and Healing

1 Marlène Kanaan, 'Legends, Places and Traditions Relating to the Cult
   of Saint George in Lebanon', *Aram*, xx (2008), pp. 203–19, at p. 213.
2 Ibid., p. 211.
3 Musa as a name is associated with Moses in Islamic tradition, although it
   is unclear whether this Musa is the same man, as the parallel legend does
   not occur in writings associated with Moses. It is worth noting, however,
   that a very similar story is associated with Elijah, who teaches Rabbi
   Joshua Ben Levi under very similar conditions – Elijah carries out a
   number of apparently outrageous acts which Joshua is unable to refrain
   from commenting on. This serves to underline the identification of
   Elijah and Al-Khidr as two forms of the same archetype.
4 Beryl Rowland, *Animals with Human Faces: A Guide to Animal Symbolism*
   (Knoxville, TN, 1973), p. 69, citing John Brand, *Observations on Popular
   Antiquities* (Newcastle, 1777).
5 Personal communication with Dan Koski, November 2012.
6 From Ida Darlington, ed., 'St George's Fields: Enclosure and
   Development', in *Survey of London xxv: St George's Fields (The Parishes of
   St George the Martyr Southwark and St Mary Newington)* (London, 1955),
   pp. 49–64. Available at www.british-history.ac.uk, accessed 30 September
   2012.

5 St George as a Dragon-slayer

1 It is notable that Chinese dragons have a much more benevolent
   cast: they have associations with rain and fertility rather than acting
   as harbingers of doom and disaster as European dragons have a
   tendency to do. I sense that this is due to the imposition of the name
   'dragon' onto these creatures of Chinese myth – essentially an act of
   mistranslation that confuses two fairly distinct concepts – one positive,
   one negative.
2 Bestiaries were mainly produced in England in the twelfth century, and
   were often made for religious houses. A good example of the form,
   the Aberdeen Bestiary, can be seen online, complete with extensive
   discussion, at www.abdn.ac.uk/bestiary, accessed 26 November 2014.
3 I have yet to see any image of a dragon where the 'orifice' is a bloody,
   fresh wound, or where the hero is attacking the dragon in this area.

But if such an image does exist, it would be very difficult to resist reading it as a representation of sexual, or sexualized, violence.

4 Respectively they are the patrician Hans Paumgarner, or Baumgartner, in the altarpiece known as the *Baumgartner Retable* (1502–4), and Emperor Maximilian in an engraving of 1508. Both images are in Munich.

5 Gerrard de Malynes, *Saint George for England, Allegorically Described* (London, 1601).

6 The simple fact of these requirements, and the implication that all members were to have access to a horse, rightly described as the Porsche of the medieval age, and be able to afford the livery, tells us a great deal about the social and economic status of the members of the guild. It is unlikely that many of them ever needed to draw down the pension that was offered to members in case of poverty.

7 Jennifer Fellows, 'St George as Romance Hero', *Reading Medieval Studies*, XIX (1993), pp. 27–54, at p. 29.

8 P. Williamson, 'The Quay to Success: Developing an Eighteenth Century Port', in *Aspects of Lancaster*, ed. S. Wilson (Barnsley, 2001), pp. 27–40. Grateful thanks to Matthew Town for bringing this discussion to my attention.

9 Jenny Uglow, *The Lunar Men* (London, 2002), p. 420.

10 *Ælfric's Lives of Saints*, vol. I, trans. and ed. W. W. Skeat, Early English Text Society OS 76 (1881), p. 5.

11 The bust of St George is one of a number of variants of a piece called *La France*, a title which is also used as an alternative appellation for this work. This underlines the ambivalent gendering of the piece and also emphasizes the likelihood that for Rodin this saint was not particularly linked to England.

6 St George and England: A Re-emerging Relevance?

1 Personal communication with Joe Townsend, October 2012.

2 John Constable, 'George and the Dragon Rap', from *The Southwark Mysteries* (London, 1999, revd edn 2011); the quoted element is reproduced by kind permission of the author and Oberon Books.

3 Personal communication with John Constable, April 2013.

4 *Saint George and Saint Patrick; or, the Rival Saintesses. An Epic Poem of the Eighteenth Century* (Dublin, 1800).

5 The title of Okri's poem is in itself a reference to William Blake's poem which begins 'And did those feet in ancient time', first published *c.* 1808. Set to music by Sir Hubert Parry in 1916 under the title 'Jerusalem', it sometimes acts as an official national anthem for England. The pertinent lines are: 'I will not cease from Mental Fight, / Nor shall my Sword sleep in my hand: / Till we have built Jerusalem, / In England's green and pleasant land.' Meanwhile, Mental Fight Club's name also contains a nod to the film *Fight Club* (dir. David Fincher, 1999, based on the

novel of the same name by Chuck Palahniuk, 1996), which centres on
a secret bare-knuckle boxing club. Its creed starts with the line 'You do
not talk about Fight Club.' By contrast, in Southwark, the motto is 'Tell
everyone about Mental Fight Club.'

6 Personal communication with Sarah Wheeler & Thomas Tobias,
April 2013.

7 Personal communication with Nicola Moss, September 2012.

8 'Bitter at the George' is published in the Ver Poets Open Competition
prize anthology, 2013 (St Albans, 2013). It is reproduced here by kind
permission of the author.

9 In fact, Cazalet has informed me that he chose to represent St George as
black as a response to the situation he perceived in Manchester without
any conscious knowledge of the 'authenticity' of presenting him in this
way: personal communication with Mark Cazalet, October 2012; a short
video of rehearsals from the Royal Opera House production of the opera,
which draws on the mumming tradition, is available as 'Backstage: *Down
by the Greenwood Side* Backstage Rehearsal', www.youtube.com, accessed
10 May 2014. Wela Mbusi was known as Wela Frasier at the time of this
production.

10 Personal communication with Joseph Payne, July 2014; grateful thanks
to Matthew Ball of the Harris Museum, Preston, for his assistance in
procuring the photographs on pp. 131.

11 Personal communication with Nicola Moss, September 2012.

Conclusion: Where Next for St George?

1 Simon Roberts, *We English* (London, 2009).

2 Roberts has informed me that the framing of this image had little
to do with any conscious decision to eliminate St George – he also
photographed a battle re-enactment, which is out of shot to the right,
but the composition around the castle's keep was more interesting
(personal communication with Simon Roberts, April 2012). However,
a postmodernist reading would certainly allow for the viewer's
interpretation to be just as valid as the creator's.

3 Paul Campbell, 'England's World Cup Shirt: Would You Pay £90
or £60 for It?', *The Guardian* (31 March 2014), www.theguardian.com.

4 U. A. Fanthorpe, 'Not my Best Side', first published in the poetry journal
Encounter, ed. Anthony Thwaite and Melvin Lasky (1975).

5 Personal communication with David Pedder, April 2014.

6 A. J. Wensinck, 'Al-Khidr', in *The Encyclopaedia of Islam*, vol. IV, new edn
(Leiden, 1976), p. 905.

BIBLIOGRAPHIC ESSAY

There is an extensive and growing bibliography on St George and his cult, but much of what is readily available has a deficiency of one sort or another so readers should ensure that their critical faculties are well honed. Anglophone authors have a marked tendency to focus on the cult in England with little or no reference to the international context (a gap that this book aims to begin to fill). Likewise there is a strong emphasis on looking for 'historical truth', especially around the question of whether St George was a real person, and it is quite common for authors to state specific dates for events in the development of the cult as if they are undisputed facts, for example, the issue of when the saint came to be recognized as the patron of the English. In my view this focus on what are effectively unanswerable questions is an unfortunate diversion away from much richer and more rewarding aspects of this very special figure.

The most useful, and by some margin the most academically rigorous, book on St George in English in the recent past is Jonathan Good, *The Cult of St George in Medieval England* (Woodbridge, 2009). The title is rather misleading, for the book is really only about the late medieval cult of this saint – not least because there is very little evidence of a cult worthy of the name in England before the Norman Conquest. Good also extends his discussion into the post-medieval era; sadly he is rather less well informed about this period than the late Middle Ages: for instance, he overlooks the multicultural and multi-faith credentials of St George in what is generally a sombre analysis of the future role of the saint as a national patron. It is to be hoped that Good will rectify this omission in further publications since he has much to offer as an analyst and commentator on the cult: despite these reservations about the scope of the work I feel that this book is a must for any serious scholar of the saint.

The other significant modern analyses of St George are not available in English. Nevertheless, they are well worth seeking out for they offer an approach which is refreshingly removed from Anglophone parochialism. The best work is perhaps Sigrid Braunfels-Esche's *Sankt Georg: Legend, Verehrung, Symbol* (Munich, 1976); more narrowly focused, but including some intriguing commentary from practising creative artists, is Georges Didi-Huberman et al., *Saint Georges et le*

Dragon: versions d'une legend (Paris, 1994). Readers might also like to be aware of my previous forays into this field, especially *St George: Hero, Martyr and Myth* (Stroud, 2000; new edn 2005) – if nothing else, I can confidently assert that the illustrations are good.

Earlier works in English which are still of some interest include Elizabeth O. Gordon, *St George* (London, 1907); Margaret H. Bulley, *St George for Merrie England* (London, 1908); Cornelia Steketee Hulst, *St George of Cappadocia in Legend and History* (London, 1909); G. J. Marcus, *Saint George of England* (London, 1929); Isabel Hill Elder, *George of Lydda: Soldier, Saint and Martyr* (Bishop Auckland, 1949); David Scott Fox, *Saint George: The Saint with Three Faces* (Oxford, 1983). To a greater or lesser extent these works all reflect some aspects of the international cult of the saint, and are also useful as indicators of the context of interest in St George in their own time of publication – the number of books on the topic in English dating from the period between the Boer War and the middle of the twentieth century is quite remarkable.

Going back well over 200 years, a still significant article is Samuel Pegge, 'Observations on the History of St George, the Patron Saint of England', *Archaeologia*, V (1779), pp. 1–32. Pegge was the first commentator to disentangle St George from the similarly named heretical bishop and pork-seller George of Cappadocia – detractors of St George still parade this misidentification today. More recent articles of significance include J. Lewis André, 'Saint George the Martyr, in Legend, Ceremonial, Art, etc.', *Archaeological Journal*, LVII (1900), pp. 204–23; Ethel Carleton Williams, 'Mural Paintings of St George in England', *Journal of the British Archaeological Association*, 3rd ser., XII (1949), pp. 19–38; Benjamin R. McRee, 'Religious Gilds and Civic Order: The Case of Norwich in the Late Middle Ages', *Speculum*, LXVII (1992), pp. 69–97; Jennifer Fellows, 'St George as a Romance Hero', *Reading Medieval Studies*, XIX (1993), pp. 27–54; Miriam Gill, '"Now help, St George, oure lady knight . . . to strengthe our Kyng and England right": Rare Scenes of Saint George in a Wall Painting at Astbury, Cheshire', *Transactions of the Lancashire and Cheshire Antiquarian Society*, XCI (1995), pp. 91–102. Between them these contributions consider expressions of St George's cult, primarily in England, in literature, art and public spectacle. Fellows's edition of Richard Johnson's *Seven Champions of Christendom* (Farnham, 2003) is also well worth seeking out.

In addition to these sound academic expositions, St George, more than many other saints, attracts a fair amount of interest from writers on the further reaches of enquiry. The approach of these commentators is usually informed by J. G. Frazer's *The Golden Bough* (London, 1933), especially in their consideration of what can be broadly termed 'folk tradition'. Paul Broadhurst's *The Green Man and the Dragon: The Mystery Behind the Myth of St George and the Dragon Power of Nature* (Launceston, 2006) provides a diverting but far from uncontroversial analysis, linking St George to ancient Egypt, megalithic temples and the Knights Templar, among other topics. A rather more restrained approach is provided by John Heath-Stubbs, 'The Hero as Saint: St George', in *The Hero in Tradition and Folklore*, ed. H.R.E. Davidson, The Mistletoe Series XIX (London, 1984), pp. 1–15.

The focus of Bob Stewart's *Where is Saint George? Pagan Imagery in English Folksong* (London, 1977) is similarly beyond the pale of much academic study, though it arguably fits quite neatly with the discussion of folk traditions presented in Eddie Cass and Steve Roud, *Room, Room, Ladies and Gentlemen: An Introduction to the English Mummers' Play* (London, 2002) – the texts and analysis presented here provide good evidence of one specific aspect of the ongoing role of St George in English culture which is often beyond the reach of 'conventional' academic investigation. Many academics foreswear dabbling in these murky waters, but braver souls will find a wealth of material and argument, some of which may prove to be surprisingly compelling in light of European comparatives – although, as with more conventional analyses, swallowing these authors' theses wholesale is never recommended.

ACKNOWLEDGEMENTS

This book came into being thanks to Ben Hayes of Reaktion, who caught me at a weak moment and persuaded me that I really shouldn't miss the opportunity to write a study of St George that focused on the lively contemporary and international cult of this hugely significant figure. Behind it there is the better part of twenty years of ongoing research which has been fitted around a series of jobs and commitments. A wide range of individuals, drawn from disparate countries and peoples, and many faith traditions, have contributed to my work over this period. Some of them have corresponded with me by email or phone, others have met with me for discussions, and quite a few (too often, sadly anonymously) have asked interesting questions of me or made enlightening comments following talks I have given to school groups, universities, local historical societies and other special interest groups, and even the national conference of the Green Party of England and Wales. My thanks go out to them all – and of course I take full responsibility for all mistakes and misinterpretations that have found their way into these pages.

I would particularly like to thank the following people who have offered their knowledge, challenged my thinking, sent me images, helped with translation and supported me in a host of practical ways: Matthew Ball, Frank Battaglia, Susannah Bleakley, Maria Clara Carniero, Garth Cartwright, Mark Cazalet, Maggie Clowes and R. Ian Campbell, Chris Coates, John Constable, Denise Dent, Julia Emerson, Katja Fält, Msgr Joseph Farrugia, Jennifer Fellows, Miriam Gill, Madeleine Gray, Diane Hopkins and Andrew Okey, Dorothy Jackman, John Jenkins, Kathleen Kay and Marianella Story, Dan Koski, Jennifer Lauruol, Phillip Lindley, James McGregor, Jude Mackley, Scott Montgomery, Nicola Moss, the late John Norris, Sara Nobili-Park, Anne O'Connor, Joseph Payne, Andrew and Fi Richardson, Simon Roberts, Sarah Salih, Canon Andrew Shanks, David Shotter, Pam and Peter Sumner, Joe Townsend, Jenny Uglow, Sarah Wheeler & Thomas Tobias, Andrew White, Christine Wilkinson, Roger Wilson, Angus Winchester, Mike Winstanley, David Woods. The staff of a number of libraries, galleries and collections have assisted my researches with varying degrees of graciousness; these include the British Library, the British Museum, the Warburg Institute, the Museum of London, the Harris Museum and Art Gallery in Preston and my home institution of Lancaster University.

Special mention must go to my family. Colin Bertram has accepted and supported my frequent and sometimes lengthy absences (both physical and mental) on St George-related business, kept the home fires burning and the cat fed, helped with proofreading and tolerated a questionable number of dragon-related books and objects in the house; Kishon McGuire has proved to be an excellent travelling companion and perceptive observer, even though he must find his seventeenth year of hearing me talk about St George somewhat trying.

The two people who have done most to support me through many challenges in my academic and personal life over the past decade are my parents. With great affection, this book is dedicated to them.

PHOTO ACKNOWLEDGEMENTS

The author and publishers wish to express their thanks to the following sources of illustrative material and/or permission to reproduce it:

Photo Jenny Alexander: p. 33; photos the author: pp. 33, 36, 37, 52, 55, 61, 63, 64, 81, 119, 138; photo Susannah Bleakley: pp. 6, 44, 46 top and bottom; British Library, London: p. 87; © Trustees of the British Museum, London: p. 49; photo Mark Cazalet: p. 115; courtesy of the Harris Museum and Art Gallery, Preston, and Simon Critchley of Museum Photography North West: p. 131; photo Michael Leaman: p. 47; courtesy Philip Lindley: p. 105; photo Nicola Moss: p. 133; National Gallery, London: p. 125; Svetlana Petrova: p. 139; © Simon Roberts: p. 137; Royal Collection, Windsor: p. 111; © Victoria & Albert Museum, London: p. 31.

INDEX